BALANCING THE

MW00941317

Visit the author's website: www.braziliankidskare.org

Library of Congress Cataloging-in-Publication Data: 2015

International Standard Book Number:

E-book International Standard Book Number:

Table of Contents

Introduction

In this book, we will learn how to begin and become effective in the prophetic ministry. Every believer should become active in this important ministry and be used in prophesying on a regular basis. It is important to understand that the gift of prophecy is not a toy, but a tool to equip, edify, and bless the church. I believe that every Christian should function in all the different ministries. According to Ephesians 4, God gave five different gifts to the church.

> *And He Himself gave some to be apostles, some prophets, some evangelists, and some pastors and teachers, for the equipping of the saints for the work of ministry, for the edifying of the body of Christ.*
> —EPHESIANS 4:11–12

These five ministries have a very specific purpose. The main purpose of the New Testament prophet is *not* to prophesy, although this is part of the ministry. The main purpose is to equip the Christians to do so. If this is done effectively, the whole church will be edified and built up. If all five ministries equip the church, every Christian will move in all five gifts, and the church will become a strong and victorious body of believers. I believe when the body of Christ learns to activate the prophetic ministry and use it properly, we will achieve more with less energy. True prophetic ministry will impart grace to people and set them free to become what God wants them to be. It will give them hope and show them the way ahead.

I trust that through this material the saints will be equipped and learn to move in a healthy and balanced way in the prophetic ministry.

—REINHARD HIRTLER

CHAPTER 1

Tools Not Toys

My Painful Experience

For more than 35 years I have been involved in the prophetic ministry. In those decades of serving Jesus, I have travelled to and preached in countless churches in many different nations of the world. God has graciously allowed me to teach and train many people in the prophetic ministry, which I consider a special grace and privilege from the Lord towards me. I have seen all the extremes, abuses, as well as fears regarding the prophetic ministry that you can possibly imagine.

About 25 years ago, I was traveling home from one of the churches we planted in the south of Austria. I spent most of the 3-hour drive in the car alone praying and trying to work through my own disappointment with the prophetic ministry. In Austria, the churches were small and almost all of them were extremely religious and legalistic, and the prophetic ministry basically did not exist when we started out. We were young and I was thrown into this ministry without ever desiring it or asking for it. In fact, I would have preferred to have had nothing to do with it at all and just been a nice pastor and church planter. But I felt I had no choice and if I wanted to obey God, I had to embrace that calling. Of course, I did have the choice to be disobedient to the calling. So we planted one church after another with mostly newly converted people.

The first town we went to had about 22,000 inhabitants and there was not one single Christian in that town that we could find. As soon as people got saved, I began to train them in the prophetic. Our churches were well known for the regular, active operation of the prophetic gift among us. It was as normal as it is to sing worship songs in a service. However, as I was driving home that Sunday, as mentioned above, I told the Lord that I would forsake the prophetic ministry and simply be a church planter and pastor.

I felt deeply disappointed and frustrated with what I saw in our own churches that I myself had trained in the prophetic ministry. Church members started to manipulate other people in different ways and were abusing the "*gift of prophecy"*. One engaged couple was prophesied to by another member that did not agree with their relationship, saying that he saw a vision in which the wedding rings were broken, and God was telling them they must not get married, otherwise they will end up in divorce. All sorts of different abuses began to take place. As I explain in a later chapter, I also saw many people aborting their prophecies.

I was not the pastor of the church, because after we planted it we assigned each church their own pastor, but I felt so frustrated and responsible for the mess, because when we planted the church, I was the one who had trained those people. I knew the abuse was not my fault, but I loved the people and saw the pain the gift, which I taught them to operate in, was causing. I told the Lord that never again will I prophesy, and I was done with the prophetic ministry. In my wrestling with the Lord on that drive home, He began to speak to my heart. He told me that I must not give up on that ministry but teach and instruct the people the proper way to handle prophecy.

Tools not Toys

One of the things that I began to understand was that the gift of prophecy is like a knife. You can use a knife to kill people. This does not make the knife a bad thing at all. In fact, knives do not kill people at all; people who abuse knives kill people. You can use a knife correctly and cut a beautiful piece of meat, which you just grilled. How would we enjoy our good barbeque without that wonderful tool of a knife? We even teach little children how to use knives correctly, yet knives still kill people. No responsible parent would throw out all knives from their household just because someone used a knife to kill somebody. Yet I have met pastors all over the world who have done just that with the gift of prophecy. They saw the abuse and stopped the gift from flowing in their churches. I almost became one of those pastors. Prophecy is not a toy we use to play with, it is a tool we so desperately need in the body of Christ.

I have seen this gift used as a tool and change thousands of lives all over the world. I have seen whole churches changed through this precious tool, as well as the lives of people saved from death and destruction. It is not the gift of prophecy that is the problem. How is it used? Is it used as a tool or as a toy to play with, or to boost our ego and then progress from there onto hurting people with it because our playing gets out of control? This tool must always be seen as just that, a tool, and used humbly and lovingly. We must always be willing to be corrected when we use it.

Biblical Guidelines

There is a very simple guideline, that if taught and followed, every church can feel safe with this gift. Many churches have abandoned scriptural guidelines and so have thrown out the baby with the bathwater. *(Daniel, if you don't have this idiom or a similar one, just change it to what I am trying to say)*. By throwing out prophecy, they have robbed many people of tremendous blessings and hindered the growth and edification of the church. I will talk later about these clear guidelines, but just to help you understand, I will briefly mention them here. We are told in 1 Corinthians 14:3 what prophecy is for:

> *But he who prophesies speaks edification and exhortation and comfort to men.*

Here we see three clear words, and all New Testament prophecy must contain these three things, or at least one of them, and must *never* go against it. These three words have the meaning to edify, to encourage and to comfort. If we understand this, all fear of abuse of prophecy will cease to exist.

The Three Sources

There can only be three sources for the gift of prophecy: the devil, our flesh or the Spirit of God. Let me ask a simple question. Does the devil ever want to edify you, encourage you or comfort you? The answer is clearly NO!!! He will always try to do the opposite, so he can be ruled out as the source of all New Testament prophecy, if we stick to the biblical guidelines for prophesying. The next question is, could it be your flesh? The answer is a clear yes! Of course, you could prophesy thinking it is the Spirit of God, yet it was coming from your own mind. Again, if we are true to the guidelines of 1 Corinthians 14:3, then nobody will get harmed, because edification, encouragement and comfort do not harm people. They will know in their own spirit that it was not a word from God, but from your own well-meaning mind and soul. This is how we learn, only by practicing. Everyone has the right to test the prophecy received. I explain this in more detail in a later chapter.

Do not put it on the Shelf

Lastly, do not put a prophecy that you have received on the shelf or in your drawer and let it get all dusty while ignoring it. God speaks to us for a purpose. Tools are to be used, not hidden like the man in the parable who had the one talent hid his. I have received many prophecies during my lifetime. I always take them very seriously. When God speaks, I write it down; I carry them in my heart like Mary the mother of Jesus did (Luke 2:19). I regularly read and align my life according to them and prayerfully ask the Holy Spirit to help me apply these prophecies. God never wastes any word which He speaks, whether through the Bible or through prophesy. Of course, you must be sure that it was a true word from God. God has called us to be co-workers with Him in His kingdom and prophecies have a very important part in His big plan.

Chapter 2

Hearing God's Voice

Before we look at what the Bible says about prophesying and who can prophesy, we need to ask the question, "How we can learn to hear God's voice?" Without hearing the voice of God, we will not be able to prophesy because we can only say what God says if we have learned to hear His voice accurately.

God's Desire to Communicate

It has always been the desire of God to communicate with His children. As we study the Bible, we will see that God spoke often. He spoke to Noah, Abraham, and Joseph in Genesis; to Moses in the midst of the burning bush in Exodus; and to the children of Israel throughout their journey in the wilderness, and to Joshua at the verge of the Promised Land. Throughout the Old Testament, God constantly spoke to His people. In Exodus, God gave very clear and detailed instructions to Moses to build Him a tabernacle because He desired to dwell among His people.

God has always desired to be close to His children and communicate with them.

> *And let them make Me a sanctuary, that I may dwell among them.*
>
> —EXODUS 25:8

Many metaphors that the Bible uses for the relationship between us and God clearly suggest an active communication. He is our bridegroom, our Father. We are His co-laborers, His soldiers… All of these metaphors indicate a clear and constant communication.

The Great Lie

Some Christians believe that God only speaks to some especially called and anointed people. They believe that only these "special" people can hear clearly from God, and the rest of the Christians have to find these people in order to receive a word from God or a prophecy. This is a lie and completely unbiblical. The Bible teaches quite the opposite:

> *But you are a chosen generation, a royal priesthood, a holy nation, His own special people, that you may proclaim the praises of Him who called you out of darkness into*

His marvelous light; who once were not a
people but are now the people of God, who
had not obtained mercy but now have
obtained mercy.

—1 PETER 2:9–10

This is written to the church and not to some special people. Every member of the true church of Jesus Christ who is born again is part of a very special royal priesthood. The various members and ministries have different functions, but nobody is more special to God. We are all His very special people.

Some Christians believe that they are not worthy to hear from God. They believe that they first have to earn something or do something special. We have not been made worthy because of anything that we have done or will ever do, but only because of the finished work of Jesus Christ on the cross of Calvary.

The Words of Jesus

Jesus Himself said in John 10:2–3 that His sheep hear His voice:

But he who enters by the door is the shepherd of the sheep. To him the doorkeeper opens, and the sheep hear his voice; and he calls his own sheep by name and leads them out.

If we are the sheep of Jesus and He is our shepherd, then we are all able to hear His voice. So often we as Christians make a great mistake. When the Bible doesn't match up with our experience, we try to explain it or just ignore it. Even worse, we try to adapt the Bible to fit our lives. We must not do that; rather, we must adapt our lives to the Word of God. Jesus clearly states that His sheep are able to hear His voice. He doesn't say that only His mature sheep, who have developed into good leaders, can hear His voice; He simply said that His sheep are able to hear His voice. Every Christian has the ability to hear God's voice.

The Word Became Flesh

The Bible says in John 1:14 that when Jesus came to this Earth, He not only spoke words from God, but He actually was the very Word of God who became flesh for us. This clearly shows the desire of God to communicate with us. He did not just send Jesus to speak to His people, He sent the

Word from heaven and made it take on human flesh, so strong was His desire to communicate His heart to the people.

It is very important that, when we learn to prophesy and hear from God, we do not just seek information, but we feel and understand His heart. God loves to speak, but He doesn't just want to give us information; He wants to communicate His heart to us. True prophetic people, who have matured in their gift, will always communicate the heart of God. When I began to be used by God in the prophetic ministry in the '80s, I felt God speak clearly to me that He would never give me a prophecy just to make a great atmosphere in a meeting or to make me look good; He would give me a prophetic word because He loves His people and His church. He told me I must always seek to communicate His heart and edify the church with the prophetic gift.

How to Hear God's Voice

Just like in any relationship, communication must be developed. Here are some important principles that will help us to develop the ability to hear God's voice better. Notice I said *"to develop the ability.*" Hearing God's voice is not a skill that we learn, but an ability that we must develop. Since we are all born again, our spirit is now alive and is able to communicate with our heavenly Father. We communicate through our spirit, which is an ability that must be developed. Often our soul has been so dominant and loud that the ears of our heart are dull; nevertheless, we have the ability. Now we must learn to develop it. We must pursue our relationship with God above all things and take time to develop a strong love relationship with Him.

Chapter 3

Communication

If you read these following words with a religious attitude, or with the eyes of the law or the old covenant, these words will not be helpful to you; they will bring you into bondage, rather than into freedom. What I am teaching you here is not a way to impress God, convince Him to love you or use you more. I am not talking about something legalistic, but rather an invitation to respond to His amazing grace and deep love for us in a way that will cause us to live in a very intimate and wonderful love relationship with Him, so that we can always hear and distinguish His voice quickly and clearly from any of the many other voices which constantly flood our lives. Jesus did not die to bring us religion; He died to restore us to a perfect love relationship with our Father, who is love.

Since I was very young, I have not only loved God, but have always had a deep desire to be in an active love relationship with Him. I have pursued this relationship since childhood.

Naturally, if we want to be in a love relationship with anyone, communication is a very important part. There can be no good relationship unless there is good communication. Just think about any relationship that you have. If it is meaningful, there will also be good, open communication where people share their hearts with each other, give each other their full attention, and truly listen to each other.

It was very early in our marriage and we had been so busy serving Jesus that we had had very little time for each other for quite a while. My wife desired to just have a few hours with me. So we found the time where just the two of us could be alone without our children. As she began to talk and open her heart, I sat and listened to her intently. At least that is what I had thought; my heart and my mind were elsewhere. Then suddenly she said: *"You are not listening to me."*

I assured her that I was and because of a very good memory that God has blessed me with, I repeated the last three sentences back to her quoting perfectly word for word. Her reply was: *"But you are still not listening to me"*! I wanted to argue, but was rebuked by the Holy Spirit, when He told me: "*You are only listening to her words, but not to her heart*". That radically changed our communication until this day. I understood that Debi was after a heart relationship and did not just want someone who would listen only to her words.

Removing distractions

But not only did my wife and my communication skills change that day, that experience also deeply impacted my relationship with the Lord. The Lord continued to speak to me and told me how it displeased Him too when I listen to Him halfheartedly. He doesn't want me to come into His presence like a spoiled teenager just grabbing something from Him and then going my own way.

His love for us will never change; it is way too deep even for our minds to ever grasp this truth. Even though He will always love us deeply and unconditionally, there are things in our lives that please Him and other things that displease Him. One of the things that displease Him is when we do not give Him our full attention when we come into His presence in order to spend time with Him.

A big part of the prophetic ministry and of prophesying is listening. In order to be able to truly listen to God, we must remove distractions from our lives. We live in a very fast paced world and most people are driven today by so many things they *have* to do. Never have people worked so few hours, yet been so stressed and so rushed. Something has gone wrong somewhere. Just two generations ago, when my grandparents were working, a normal workweek was about 60 hours. One generation ago when my parents worked, it was over 50 hours a week. A normal workweek today is much less. I understand that people work overtime, but so did my parents and grandparents.

What does all this have to do with the prophetic and especially with hearing the voice of God, you may ask? It has everything to do with it. One of the reasons we find it so hard to listen to the voice of God is because we listen to so many other voices on a constant basis. We are connected 24/7 with the whole world through our technical gadgets and the social media. We have thousands of friends, but often have no time for true friendship and communion with the Holy Spirit. If we truly want to move in the prophetic and become sensitive to the voice of the Holy Spirit, we must remove distractions from our lives, at least at the times we are trying to spend in His presence.

I remember once when I was praying, I said to the Holy Spirit that I want Him to be my very best friend. He immediately replied: "*I am, but I want you to be my best friend too*". It hit my heart like a lightning bolt. Ever since then I asked Him hundreds of times to help me and to teach me how to become His best friend. This began a journey in my life that has probably been the most difficult yet the most wonderful thing in my Christian life. It brought more drastic and significant change to my life than any other experience I have ever had with God.

It has been the most difficult in that my life is very busy and there are always many things that I have to do. It is impossible to develop an intimate relationship with anybody unless you specifically set apart time for them. When you are goal-driven, like I am, it becomes very difficult to spend hours silently in the presence of the Holy Spirit.

It has become the most wonderful thing in that His presence is the sweetest and most invigorating thing that one can ever experience. In His presence frustrations, physical, spiritual and emotional tiredness just melts away. His presence changes our character effortlessly. When His voice permeates our spirit it affects every fiber of our being.

There are too many things that are involved in friendship with the Holy Spirit that I cannot write about it all here. We need to learn to become familiar with the voice of the Spirit in order to truly be flowing in the prophetic gift, because prophesying means to hear and then speak what God/His Spirit is saying. That is why we need to spend time learning to hear His voice.

Often people are impressed with how the Holy Spirit speaks through me so accurately and detailed, and they think it has to do with my calling of being a prophet. I am sure that partially has something to do with it, but that is, in fact the lesser part of it; the greater part has to do with my intimacy with the Lord Jesus, the Father and His Holy Spirit.

How often do we spend time in prayer or read the Bible and have our cell phones in our pockets or on our laps on silent or vibrate mode? We keep being interrupted by their vibrating, responding to the world's beckoning, often only with a quick glance, though we should have set this time apart for *undivided* fellowship with the Lord. Instead of removing this particular distraction from our lives for a short period of time, we respond to it and so are unable to truly focus on the voice of the Holy Spirit.

I remember so well when that also used to be the normal habit of my daily life. I got up in the morning and made myself a cup of hot tea. While I was waiting for the water to boil I was checking my messages on the phone. Then I grabbed my Bible, my tea and my cell phone and began to read the Bible and pray. As I was doing this one-day, the phone was on silent mode as always, but it was constantly disturbing me with new messages coming in. I quickly glanced every few minutes, and then got so frustrated with it and told the Lord, that this cell phone is such a curse.

He replied: "*No, it is a great blessing that I want you to use. You are the one who has turned this great blessing into a curse by misusing it.*" He then continued to talk to me about how to use it correctly and what the results would be if I would obey. It was one of the greatest battles of my life. I had no idea how addicted I was to such a small electronic device and how I had turned it from a blessing into a curse in my own life.

The saddest thing in all this was, that I allowed it to distract me from communion with my sweet Jesus, and the Holy Spirit, whose voice I love to hear. Once I established the habit that He taught me, that in the morning not to turn it on nor even look at it until I had spent at least 90 undistracted minutes in His presence, my life radically changed. Shortly afterwards the anointing, the authority and the miracles increased. I had that same anointing and authority before but it was just that I was unable to tap into it because of my own foolishness in allowing myself to be distracted from giving Him my full and undivided attention first thing in the morning. The abuse and misuse of our phones and other electronic devices has become so normal, that we are not even aware of what we are doing to ourselves.

This abuse of electronics and any negative outcome in our lives has nothing to do with God withholding anything from us. Through Christ we have been given full authority, anointing and access to the entire supernatural world. However, we are the ones who do not access these things because our hearts and minds have been drawn away from His sweet presence. It is in spending time with the Holy Spirit that our hearts will receive or will be filled with the revelation of what already belongs to us which, in turn will affect every area of our lives.

The attitude and behavior of letting anything disturb or interrupt our time or fellowship with the Lord must change if we want to experience all that God has for us. We have some of the most powerful Bible teachers today that we are able to learn from. Yet how little does the Word of God, which comes through these anointed channels, affect our lives, because we only half-heartedly listen to the wonderful revelations they are sharing with us?

Again, please understand and hear my heart. You can do with your cellphone, laptop, iPad, and Internet whatever you want to, it is your personal decision. But would it not be so much more beneficial, that when the Word of God is preached, or when we are reading it or spending personal one-on-one time with Him that we remove all distractions from our lives and give Him our undivided attention, desiring to learn from Him, listening intently and being changed by Him?

Chapter 4

Relaxing in His Presence

We can only give what we have, and we only have what we first received. We have nothing from ourselves; we came into this world naked and with empty hands. Therefore, in order to prophesy we must first receive a revelation from the Holy Spirit so that we can pass it on.

The first law of life is receiving, not giving. The body needs to breathe in and out in order to be healthy. Many Christians only breathe out without breathing in, spiritually speaking, and do not even realize that this is what they are doing. They are never fruitful and they do not know why. We must first breathe in, which means, first comes the receiving. In our Christian life we have to learn to relax in God's presence and breathe in His energy, strength, wisdom, love and His Word etc.

Breathing out, spiritually speaking, is also very important. Problems occur, when people either just breathe in, or just breathe out. The ones who just breathe in are the Christian mystics. They spend their whole life away from people *"just in the presence of God in meditation and prayer*" yet never do anything for humanity. This is as bad as just breathing out without breathing in. The Dead Sea has no life in it. One of the reasons for this is because water flows into it but no water ever flows out of it.

We need to learn to be still in the presence of God, enjoy His fellowship without any distractions and hear His voice daily. But then we need to do something with what God has shared with us from His heart. We need to share these revelations with other people. We need to help others, prophesy to others and let the life and power of God flow through our lives. Learning to hear from God just so that we can be excited about all the revelations we receive makes us just like the Dead Sea. We need to learn to hear His voice for ourselves, but also in order to prophesy to the people so they can be edified.

Few Christians have learned the secret of relaxing in the presence of God. Their prayer life is all about talking to God and asking Him for things they need or want from Him. A body that is not relaxed cannot receive. This is why many people do not receive a healing miracle. They are so tense that they are unable to receive what God has for them.

It is the same way with our minds and hearts. If we deliberately set time apart to practice God's presence but our minds and hearts are so overloaded with many cares, troubles or just plain distractions, which we constantly allow to disturb us, our hearts will be unable to hear the voice of God, even though He is speaking to us.

When I spend time with God, I make sure that I relax so that I can hear His voice clearly. Some people like some gentle worship music to help them draw closer to God; that helps some people to relax; I personally do not like music when I am fellowshipping with God. It is just my personal preference. In my many years of walking with Jesus, I have learned the secret of relaxing in His presence without any music or any other kind of help. I am not saying we should not have music, I am just saying I personally prefer to spend time in His presence in total quietness.

I have a very comfortable chair I sit in. I close the door to the room; I sit in a relaxing posture and I tell my body and mind to relax in God's presence. When all sorts of distracting thoughts come, I do not fight them, I simply let them come and go and constantly redirect my mind to Jesus. In order to be receptive, we *must* learn to relax. It might take time for you to learn this habit but it is well worth the time and effort.

Remember, only a relaxed body is a receptive body; only a relaxed mind is a receptive mind and only a relaxed heart is a heart that can distinguish and hear the voice of God. Before we are able to give we have to receive. You cannot breathe out until you have first breathed in. Do not spend your life in all busy-ness trying to serve God, until you have learned to relax in His presence and received from Him. Breath in the life of God, breathe in the presence of God and enjoy His presence as you relax every part of your body, mind and heart.

Leaving and Entering

Let me share another secret that I have learned, which has been a major key for my fruitful life and prophetic ministry. It is so simple, yet so few people seem to have learned it. It is the principle of leaving and entering. How you leave is always how you enter. How a baby leaves the womb of its mother is how it enters life. If it leaves the womb healthy, it enters life healthy, if it leaves the womb unhealthy or even handicapped, it enters life the same way.

How you leave this Earth is how you will enter eternal life. If you leave this Earth reconciled with God through Jesus Christ that is how you will enter eternal life. If you leave here unreconciled with God that is also how you will enter eternal life. You cannot change your choice after you have left. Once you have left this life, you have to live with whatever choice you made before you left. You will enter the same way into eternal life, either reconciled with God and enjoying eternal life with Him forever, or unreconciled with God and spending eternal life without Him.

This principle does not only apply to being born and dying, it applies to every area of our lives. If you leave one relationship in anger, you will enter the next relationship with the same anger.

When I planted our first church, people from other churches wanted to join us. Their churches were usually very dead, religious and legalistic and they usually left in much frustration. As a pastor, I did not want just any people to join our church, because I understood this principle of leaving and entering. I knew that if individuals left their church angry, frustrated and bitter, that is how they would enter our church and then they would cause many problems for themselves, me and the other members of our church. So I made sure they left their church in the right way, so that they could also enter our church in the right way. This applies to every area of our lives.

What does this have to do with the prophetic, hearing the voice of God, and relaxing in His presence? It has more to do with it than you can imagine. How you leave your day when you go to bed is how you will enter your sleep at night. How you leave your sleep in the morning is how you enter your day. I do not know about you, but I like to wake up happy, joyful, energized and full of the Holy Spirit. It is a great way to start the day. It makes it so much easier to hear the voice of God and to prophesy. It makes the day so wonderful; independent from what happens and which difficulties and tribulations one might face that day.

Since the principle of leaving and entering always works, I always make sure I leave my day right. Let me explain this to you. When I go to bed, I do not just lie down and close my eyes and go to sleep. As I get ready for bed, about 30 minutes before I go to sleep, I remove all distractions. I do not have the problem of having to turn off my TV, because we got rid of our TV about 20 years ago and never brought another one back into our lives since then. My cell phone is off and stays in another room. I read something edifying, relax my mind and heart and consciously spend time with the Lord.

I lie on my bed and spend time fellowshipping with the Lord until I eventually fall asleep. This is how I have gone to sleep every night for the past 30 years or so. What happens to me during the night? The way I left my day is the way I entered sleep. I entered it aware of the presence of the Lord. Therefore prophetic dreams are normal for me. The presence of the Lord works in my heart while I am asleep; my heart/spirit is awake and alert to His presence while my body is asleep. God never sleeps. David did this too and seemed to have understood this same principle. He says in Psalms 4:4 and 63:6

> *Meditate within your heart on your bed, and be still. When I remember You on my bed, I meditate on You in the night watches.*

I am very careful how I leave the day and enter sleep. But I am just as careful about how I leave the night as I was about how I left the day before to enter into the night. I do not get up just in time to get ready to start my day, rush out of bed and grab some breakfast and get on with my day by hurrying out the door. Remember, the way you leave your night is the way you enter your day. How do you think you will be able to hear the voice of the Holy Spirit clearly throughout your day if you have left your night the wrong way?

The great man of God, Dr. David Yongi Cho, pastor of the largest church in the world, learned this secret when he first started his ministry. One of my mentors and spiritual fathers trained and ordained Yongi Cho to the ministry. I had the privilege of learning so much from this mentor. He told me that Yongi Cho refused to spend time with anyone or do anything until he spent a good amount of time in prayer and the presence of the Lord totally undistracted. I have established this same habit almost 40 years ago and have never abandoned it.

I leave my day fellowshipping with the Lord and enter my night the same way. I am very careful how I leave my nights. I leave every night in the identical manner and enter every day the same way. As I wake up and leave my night, I leave it fellowshipping undistracted with the Lord and enter my day in like manner. I refuse to get out of bed and rush into my day. If you are willing to establish this habit, it will become easy for you to hear the voice of God, besides the many other amazing benefits you will also reap.

Chapter 5

Learning to Pray

We are told in Ephesians 6:18 that we should pray with different kinds of prayers

> ...*praying always with all prayer and supplication in the Spirit, being watchful to this end with all perseverance and supplication for all the saints*

One of the meanings in the original Greek for the word which is used here for "*all prayers*" is "*some of all types*". There are different types of prayers. Unfortunately when Christians think of prayer, most of them just think of talking to God. Because of this, many Christians rarely hear the voice of God and then falsely believe that God does not speak to them. This is far from the truth. God is a speaking God and constantly speaks to all of His children. The problem is that His children do not hear Him, because they have not learned the art of "*listening prayer*".

Prayer Based on Urgency

Let me ask you a question here. What is your first reaction when you are in a crisis, or have some trouble? Is it to pray? Most Christians respond to a crisis by praying, and think it is a noble thing to do. I personally do not agree that this should be our first reaction, at least not in the sense of how Christians usually understand praying.

They understand praying as talking to God and telling or asking Him to fix their problem. This is not my first reaction. For several reasons I believe it is not a good first reaction. Please do not hear what I am not saying. I am all for praying, and praying earnestly. However, we must understand that the Bible talks about different *kinds* of prayers; so there are prayers that are more than just talking to God and telling Him all our problems and asking Him to fix them. Here are the reasons why I think prayers that are born out of urgency are not a good response to our problems:

1. We focus on the wrong things

When our prayers are born out of urgency, the devil has an easy job to make us ineffective. As it is, life is incredibly busy for most of us. Most people do not have enough time, it seems, to fellowship with God and practice intimacy with Him. When our prayers are born out of urgency, all the devil has to do is to throw some urgent problems in our lives and we are sidetracked from what God wants us to do. Now all we do is talk to God about our problems. Our focus changes from God and His purpose to us and our problems.

2. Dictating the questions

When prayer is born out of urgency, we dictate to God the conversation which we want Him to listen to, instead of listening to His counsel and wisdom regarding our situation. Because of this attitude, we often cannot hear what God is saying to us. Urgency always starts the conversation by telling God our problems, but God wants to start the conversation with sharing His plan with us. Often His plans are very different than our ideas about the situation. He sees things from a very different perspective for several reasons. He sees the end before the beginning; He sees the solution and not just the problem. In His eyes, every problem is an opportunity to demonstrate and release the victory of the finished work of the cross in our lives. God desires to share His perspective with us, yet all we do is take control of the conversation and tell Him what we want Him to do for us, thereby missing His voice and His great plans for us. If you want to move in the prophetic, you must learn the art of listening prayer.

3. Rushing through prayer

Urgency always wants the conversation to be quick. Because we are driven by our needs and urgencies, we want to hurry up, tell God what to do and have Him quickly fix our problem. We pray intensely and think the louder and more intense we pray, the more we will convince God to listen and respond to us. This is old covenant thinking which we must get out of our minds and hearts. While urgency wants prayer to be quick, God wants to prepare our hearts to hear His voice, which usually takes time. God is far more interested in our deep, intimate relationship with Him than just quickly fixing our problems.

4. Writing God into our story

Urgency writes God into our story, which is the opposite of what God wants to do. Maybe you think this is an honorable thing to do, to get God involved in your life and have Him fix your problems. I believe that rather than trying to write God into *our* story, we need to understand that God wants to write us into *His* story. One of the most amazing and overwhelming truths that I have learned through the prophetic ministry is, that God, the author and creator of all things, has an amazing story planned. His story involves the demonstration of His wonderful glory to people from all tribes and nations. It is the most amazing story that anybody could ever imagine. Our loving Father has chosen to write us into His very own glorious story, and then He allows us to participate in it as ordinary human beings.

When I was young and was starting in the ministry of serving God, I used to pray before I had to preach: "*Lord, please help me*"! He answered my prayers and helped me every time I had to preach. One day I realized that this is not the best way to pray, so I changed my prayer to: "*Lord, please use me*"! In the first prayer, *I* was doing the job with the help of God. *I* was writing *Him* into my story. In the second prayer, I was not doing the job, but *He* was and *He* was writing me into *His* story. When I go to a meeting now, I reject all my plans and simply surrender in quietness and confidence to the Lord and let Him write *me* into *His* story.

Chapter 6

Developing the Ability to Hear God

Here are some simple keys that will help us develop the ability to hear the voice of God.

First Key: When You Pray, Don't Just Talk to God

Share your heart with God, and then ask God to speak to you. Write things down for yourself, and learn through experience where you heard God clearly and where your own thoughts spoke. Keep a journal; this will help you to learn to distinguish between your own thoughts and the voice of God. Remember, it takes time to develop this ability. Most Christians pray, but they don't learn to communicate with God, which is talking and listening.

Don't be like the couple that came to court because they wanted to get divorced. When the judge asked for the reason of their divorce, the wife said that in 19 years the husband had never told her that he loved her and she just couldn't take it anymore. When the judge asked husband if this was true, he replied that it was. In amazement, the judge asked why he never told his wife that he loved her. He replied that he had been trying to tell her for the last 19 years, but she would never be quiet and listen, so he had no chance to talk.

Second Key: Exercise Your Faith When You Come to God

God promises us in His Word that when we seek Him, we will find Him. He desires for us to seek Him with all of our hearts, and He guarantees us through His Word that if we do, we will find Him. God's promises are true; God doesn't lie. We must believe that everything He says, He also means.

> *And you will seek Me and find Me, when you search for Me with all your heart.*
> —JEREMIAH 29:13

He also promises us that when we draw near to Him, He will draw near to us.

> *Draw near to God and He will draw near to you.*

Come in faith and assurance that God is ready to listen to you and share His heart with you.

Third Key: Feel God's Heart; Don't Just Hear His Voice

When it comes to hearing God in order to be used in prophecy, we must learn something very important. Although God loves to share information with His children, He wants us to feel His heart. Remember, God is after a relationship with us, and if all we do is seek information, we will often miss the point of prophecy and can get in great danger. Prophecy is never about us—how great we look, or how wonderfully we can prophesy. It is about God communicating His heart with His people.

Once at the beginning of our marriage, my wife was talking to me and suddenly said, "You are not listening to me." I assured her that I was and quoted the last four sentences back to her perfectly. She immediately replied, "But you still are not listening to me." As I reflected on what she said, I had to admit that she was right. I had listened to her information, but never even tried to understand her heart. This has changed our communication in our marriage. In the same way, we must always try to feel the heart of God, and then we will also be able to learn to hear His voice more clearly.

Fourth Key: Focus on God Through Thanksgiving and Praise

Too often our focus is just on telling God what we need, instead of focusing on God Himself. The Bible says that the way we enter His presence is by focusing on Him. As we walk through the gates into the presence of God, we should give thanks to Him as we do so, which moves our focus away from us to Him.

> *Enter into His gates with thanksgiving, and into His courts with praise. Be thankful to Him, and bless His name.*
> —PSALM 100:4

I have found that often when I am not focused and my soul and senses scream louder than my spirit within, I simply need to shift my focus away from myself to God. Begin to praise and worship God; then quiet your soul and listen to the Spirit of God within.

Fifth Key: Pray in the Spirit

Scripture teaches us that when we pray in tongues, we *edify* ourselves. The meaning of this word is to build ourselves up; it can also have the meaning of repairing.

> *He who speaks in a tongue edifies himself,*
> *but he who prophesies edifies the church.*
> —1 CORINTHIANS 14:4

As we pray in tongues, which every believer should regularly do, our spirit is being built up and becomes more sensitive to the Spirit of God within us. Paul understood this and prayed in tongues a lot:

> *I thank my God I speak with tongues more*
> *than you all.*
> —1 CORINTHIANS 14:18

Since we hear God from within through our spirit, we need to make sure that our spirit is constantly being built up and edified. I spend much time in praying in tongues; it helps me focus from without to within and learn to hear the voice of God better.

Sixth Key: Take Time to Listen

Don't rush out of His presence as soon as you have finished your prayer. Sit quietly and wait for your spirit to hear God speak to you. When I was a child, I always wanted to help my dad repair things around the house. My dad is a very skilled craftsman and can fix anything. Often when I was helping him, he would tell me to go to the garage to get a certain tool. I was always in a hurry and ran off before he could explain to me exactly what he wanted and

where I could find it. I came back frustrated, telling him that the tool was not in the garage.

He once told me that he wanted to give me clear instruction, but I couldn't wait for him to do so; instead, I rushed away from his presence, and therefore missed what he wanted to say. This is how many Christians are with God. They pray and tell God everything; then rush out of His presence.

Seventh Key: Listen From Within, Not Without

We hear with the ears of our heart, our spirit. Our senses are just the vehicle; they give expression to our spirit. Just as you need your natural senses and your body to express love (touch, speech, etc.), you need your senses to express your spirit. But the hearing is from within. This is very important to understand. Some people teach that you should just say anything that comes to your mind—it is God speaking to you. I believe that such a belief is very dangerous because it opens us up to delusion. We then believe that everything that comes into our mind is God speaking—but, of course, there is our natural mind, our carnal thoughts, and even demonic influence.

Our mind is the battleground, and the devil will try to gain access. Therefore, we must learn to hear from our spirit, deep within us. The way of transporting the revelation will be our natural senses, such as our speech, but the origin comes from deep within, from our spirit. It must come from the Spirit of God to our spirit, which we then express through our senses. Sometimes we read the Bible, and it is good because it is God's Word; we receive it with our mind and thoughts. But we all should know that wonderful experience when the Holy Spirit uses the Bible to speak deep within our spirit; our thoughts then receive it, and our mouth declares it.

> *The spirit of a man is the lamp of the* LORD, *searching all the inner depths of his heart.*

> —PROVERBS 20:27

Our spirit is the lamp of God inside of us; it is there because God put it there. When we are born again, our spirit becomes alive and connects with God. It searches all the inner parts of our heart. Therefore, as I said earlier, we must learn to develop the ability to hear the Spirit of God within us.

When God began to use me in the gift of prophecy, I went through the same struggles all the other people I have talked to go through. The biggest problem is knowing that this is God speaking and not just our own ideas. As you begin to grow in this gift and learn to distinguish His voice from your own thoughts, don't be afraid of mistakes. Ask God for confirmation. I was so scared and always doubted myself when I began in this ministry, but I had a deep hunger for God and wanted to be used by Him desperately. I fasted and prayed, and cried and wept so much. I was so insecure. I desperately wanted to be used by God in the gift of prophecy. So I kept asking God to confirm to me that I was hearing Him and not just myself. Many times, when God gave me a prophecy and I hesitated, someone else would stand up and give the same prophecy. I felt so ashamed of my unbelief and doubt that I decided to just begin to obey God and let Him teach me and correct me. I figured I would rather make mistakes, be corrected, humble myself, and be used by God than miss this wonderful opportunity of God blessing people through my life.

Eighth Key: Take Time to Develop a Deep Relationship with God Through Prayer

I have been asked many times how I learned to flow in the prophetic and how I hear God. As mentioned before, we hear God from within—with our spirit and not with our natural, carnal mind. Because of the ministry that God has called me to, since I was a child, I have been very aware of the spiritual world and very sensitive to it. However, learning to prophesy and listen carefully to the Holy Spirit were abilities that had to be developed. When God first began to give me prophecies, I was unsure if it was God; I was very afraid and didn't speak what God spoke to me in my spirit.

But I had a deep hunger to serve God with all of my heart, and I wanted to be obedient to Him, no matter what the price. I spent much time in fasting and praying, often going for very long periods—even up to 50 days—without any food. Regularly I would take three days and go to a mountain cabin or some lonely place without any distractions, just my Bible and my determination to learn to hear God. I took no phone, no computer, and had no contact with anybody. It was just me, my Bible, and God; I shut myself away, praying and seeking God. I was so hungry for God and wanted to learn to hear Him. It was during this time that I learned to develop the ability to hear God from within my spirit.

We live in a fast-paced and busy world, where people cannot be without distractions. This is one of the great hindrances in learning to hear God and to prophesy. God speaks to our spirit, deep within, but we fill our mind with so much clutter and distractions that we cannot quiet ourselves. There are no shortcuts. We need to learn to be quiet before God; turn our cell phones *off*, not on silent mode; close down our computers; shut the door; and pray. We must learn to be quiet. Then we will develop the ability to hear Him from within our spirit.

Once a year I lead a youth camp in Poland and one in Austria. About one hundred young people come together to meet God. For one week, there are absolutely no cell phones, no computers, no internet, no electronics allowed. The people learn to put aside these distractions and listen to the Spirit of God within them. Many people today want to move in the prophetic, but are unwilling to pay the price. They try to find preachers and Bible teachers who convince them that it is so easy—just say what comes to your mind. I find this unhelpful and dangerous; I have seen too many prophecies that were not from the Spirit of God.

I understand that we live in a world where we need computers and cell phones and the internet. I am thankful to God for these wonderful tools that help us be more efficient in our work and ministries. However, they are just tools and must be used as such. If we want to learn to develop the ability to hear God, it must be from our spirit, not from our flesh or carnal mind, or worse, from a demonic source.

Ninth Key: Asking God Daily to Cleanse Your Heart

This has been my constant prayer since I was a teenager. I always ask God to search my heart and cleanse me from any selfish motives and ambitions. If we have selfish motives, we will not be able to hear God clearly because we filter what God is saying to us through our own selfish desires. His will, not ours, must be our deepest heart's desire. We must pray daily, "Lord, Your will be done." If we want to hear God but are motivated by our selfish, unsanctified desires, the prophetic gift in and through us will not be pure. Let this be your daily prayer:

> *Search me, O God, and know my heart; try me, and know my anxieties; and see if there is any wicked way in me, and lead me in the way everlasting.*
> —PSALM 139:23–24

Tenth Key: Ask God Questions

Develop an intimate relationship with God. After all, He is our Father, and we are His children. Earthly fathers love to communicate with their children. How much more does Father God love to communicate with us? After asking God your questions, sit in silence and wait for Him to speak to you. Keep a diary and get to know His voice. I keep a prayer journal and write my questions down to God; then I take time to listen and write down what I believe God is saying to me. If you do this on a regular basis, you will soon learn to distinguish between God's voice and your own thoughts. The Christian life is not just about knowledge, but about experience. As you write things down in your journal and keep track, you will find out where you wrote down your own desires and thoughts—and you will learn to discern the difference.

Eleventh Key: Keep Seeking God

Often God will speak to us a part of what He actually wants to say. He does this because He desires a relationship with us and wants us to press on and keep seeking Him. God will try to do anything to draw us into a close relationship with Himself. We need to have the attitude that Jacob had when he wrestled with God:

> *Then Jacob was left alone; and a Man wrestled with him until the breaking of day.*

Now when He saw that He did not prevail against him, He touched the socket of his hip; and the socket of Jacob's hip was out of joint as He wrestled with him. And He said, "Let Me go, for the day breaks." But he said, "I will not let You go unless You bless me!

—GENESIS 32:24–26

God loves this attitude when His children persist in drawing close to Him. Remember, when He only gives you part of an answer, He often does so because He desires for you to continue to seek Him with all of your heart.

Chapter 7

Ways in Which God Speaks

We have learned that God speaks to our spirit—but in what ways does He speak? God speaks in many different ways. Too often we limit God by expecting Him to only speak in a certain way. Even though we hear God with our spirit, He uses different ways to speak to us.

When I was a teenager, a preacher in my church preached about the prophet Elijah. He said that when God spoke to Elijah in First Kings 19:1–15, there was a storm, an earthquake, and a fire, but God was not in any of them. Then came a still, small voice, which was God speaking to Elijah. The preacher continued to say that if we want to hear God, we have to listen to the still, small voice because this is *the only way* God speaks. For many years, I believed that this was the truth and that God speaks in no other way.

As I studied the Bible, I found out that God speaks in many different ways. Scripture says that sometimes when God spoke, there was a lot of noise:

> *Then it came to pass on the third day, in the morning, that there were thunderings and lightnings, and a thick cloud on the mountain; and the sound of the trumpet was very loud, so that all the people who were in the camp trembled. And Moses brought the people out of the camp to meet with God, and they stood at the foot of the mountain. Now Mount Sinai was completely in smoke, because the LORD descended upon it in fire. Its smoke ascended like the smoke of a furnace, and the whole mountain quaked greatly. And when the blast of the trumpet sounded long and became louder and louder, Moses spoke, and God answered him by voice.*
> —EXODUS 19:16–19

Scripture also says that God speaks through dreams and visions. To some people, God speaks more through inner feelings, while to others, He speaks in totally different ways. No matter how God chooses to speak, the Bible will always have to remain our unchanging guide. Anything that contradicts what God has clearly written in His Word must be rejected.

Through these pages, I want to make us aware that God is a speaking God, and we need listening ears. Jesus said, "If anyone has ears to hear, let him hear" (Mark 4:23). We have spiritual ears and natural ears, just as we have spiritual eyes and natural eyes. If we only look and listen in the natural, we will miss God's voice often, just as the people of Israel did during the time of Jesus.

> For the hearts of this people have grown dull. Their ears are hard of hearing, and their eyes they have closed, lest they should see with their eyes and hear with their ears, lest they should understand with their hearts and turn, so that I should heal them.
> —MATTHEW 13:15

Since prophesying is about hearing what God is saying and then saying it, we first need to learn the importance of developing the ability to listen to God. Everywhere you go there are radio waves, but you can only hear them if you have a radio receiver that is tuned in to the right station.

In the same way, you need to have your spiritual receiver (your spiritual ears) tuned in to God. You need to learn to tune in to the right frequency (the voice of God).

Here are some ways in which God speaks (these are not the only ways, but I find them to be the most common).

The Bible

We should never read the Bible without asking the Holy Spirit to speak to us. The Bible is not for information; it is written so that God can speak to us through it. When we read the Bible, we should quiet our hearts and ask the Holy Spirit to speak to us. I never read my Bible for information, but for revelation—to hear God speak to my heart through the words written down in His book. Every day before I open my Bible, I ask the Holy Spirit to speak to my heart; I tell Him that I will not be satisfied until I hear Him speak to me. I read and meditate and listen to the inner voice of the Holy Spirit speaking to me through the Bible. This is also a good way to get to know the voice of God.

An Inner Feeling

We are all made differently. Everybody feels things differently. Many times we have a feeling of a danger or an uncomfortable feeling about a certain decision. As we grow in God and learn to hear Him better, we learn to listen to these feelings and discern when they are from God and when they are from our own soul. I have learned that many times God speaks to me through my feelings, and I've been protected from many dangers by listening to those feelings. Other times, we may need to make a decision about a certain thing that makes no sense to our minds, but we have an inexplicable peace inside of us. We somehow know that we should do this particular thing, even though circumstances, people, and our own mind tell us differently.

Of course, we need to understand that not every feeling is God speaking to us; we need to make sure that we are not mistaking our unsanctified emotions, fears, and unhealed wounds for the voice of God. But as we develop the ability of hearing God, we will find that often God speaks to us through an inner feeling.

An Inner Voice

An inner voice is like a thought that comes to us—but these "thoughts" originate in our spirit, not in our mind. Often they are totally unrelated to anything we have been thinking about. Many times, this inner voice cuts right through our own thoughts and resonates in our spirit. Many Christians receive prophetic words in this way, but instead of speaking them in faith, they begin to let their minds and thoughts take over, allowing themselves to be filled with doubt and fear. *Remember, we speak from our spirit, not from our mind.* As they begin to reason and listen to the voice of doubt, fear sets in, and they miss an opportunity to bless someone and release a word of prophecy. We must remember that the Spirit of God lives *inside* of us. Don't listen to all of your thoughts and think that whatever comes to your mind is God speaking. Learn to quiet your own thoughts and ask God to speak to you; then with time you will learn to distinguish when that inner voice comes from your spirit or from your own mind.

Circumstances

In Numbers 22 and 23, we read the story of the prophet Balaam, who was asked by a heathen king to curse the people of God. God made it clear that he should not do so, but the prophet Balaam tried to persuade God otherwise and finally went ahead, rebelliously planning to curse God's people. When an angel stood in his way, the donkey pushed Balaam against a wall. Through these circumstances, God was trying to speak to Balaam. Instead of recognizing God's voice through these circumstances, he beat his donkey. God will often use different circumstances to speak to us. We need to have ears to hear what God is saying through our circumstances instead of fighting them or blaming people. In the end, the angel told the prophet that the donkey had saved his life. When your circumstances don't go the way you want them to go, don't just react, take time to ask God if He is using circumstances to speak to you and get your attention.

Visions

There are levels of visions. Some visions are merely light impressions in our mind's eye. We vaguely see mental images or impressions. I have found that people who are very creative often receive prophecies from God in this way. My wife comes from several generations of artists. Because she is very creative, most of the prophetic words that she receives come to her first in the form of pictures, visions, or impressions. I, however, have no creative talent; therefore, God hardly ever speaks to me in visions. He sometimes does, but not usually.

We need to learn to hear God in the many different ways He speaks; otherwise, we will miss much of what He has to say to us. Just last week, I was praying with some friends, wonderful people. As we prayed, one lady shared a vision God had given her for me. After she shared it, the pastor who was also praying with us said he had the same vision, but he was hesitant to share it until he had heard what the lady shared. He was holding it back because he was a little unsure. I told him that I had been at a meeting that morning, and some people wanted to pray for me. A lady there had this same vision. It was very important for me. God really wanted me to hear it, but the pastor doubted it because it was just a simple vision.

"Open visions" are what I call high-level visions; some people call these trances. I have had these on occasion. In an open vision, the person actually sees the vision with their open eyes, just as if it was really happening, or as if they were watching a movie. God usually speaks in an open vision when He has a very important message to give. Peter had an open vision, and it brought the gospel to the Gentiles.

The next day, as they went on their journey and drew near the city, Peter went up on the housetop to pray, about the sixth hour. Then he became very hungry and wanted to eat; but while they made ready, he fell into a trance and saw heaven opened and an object like a great sheet bound at the four corners, descending to him and let down to the earth. In it were all kinds of four-footed animals of the earth, wild beasts, creeping things, and birds of the air.

And a voice came to him, "Rise, Peter; kill and eat." But Peter said, "Not so, Lord! For I have never eaten anything common or unclean." And a voice spoke to him again the second time, "What God has cleansed you must not call common." This was done three times. And the object was taken up into heaven again. Now while

Peter wondered within himself what this vision which he had seen meant, behold, the men who had been sent from Cornelius had made inquiry for Simon's house, and stood before the gate. And they called and asked whether Simon, whose surname was Peter, was lodging there.

While Peter thought about the vision, the Spirit said to him, "Behold, three men are seeking you. Arise therefore, go down and go with them, doubting nothing; for I have sent them."

—ACTS 10:9–20

Dreams

Throughout the Bible, we see that God spoke through dreams over and over again. God can speak through dreams in symbols that need to be interpreted, or He can speak a clear, direct message as He did to Joseph, the husband of Mary.

But while he thought about these things, behold, an angel of the Lord appeared to him in a dream, saying, "Joseph, son of David, do not be afraid to take to you

*Mary your wife, for that which is conceived
in her is of the Holy Spirit."*

—MATTHEW 1:20

*Then, being divinely warned in a dream
that they should not return to Herod, they
departed for their own country another way.*

—MATTHEW 2:12

*Now when they had departed, behold, an
angel of the Lord appeared to Joseph in a
dream, saying, "Arise, take the young
Child and His mother, flee to Egypt, and
stay there until I bring you word; for Herod
will seek the young Child to destroy Him."*

—MATTHEW 2:13

*Now when Herod was dead, behold, an
angel of the Lord appeared in a dream to
Joseph in Egypt...*

—MATTHEW 2:19

*But when he heard that Archelaus was
reigning over Judea instead of his father
Herod, he was afraid to go there. And
being warned by God in a dream, he turned
aside into the region of Galilee.*

Again, we must take caution not to believe that every dream is from God. Dreams can come from various sources—from our own fears, and from emotional difficulties and hurts we have not worked through and been healed of. We are told in Ecclesiastes that there are natural sources for a dream too: "For a dream comes through much activity" (Eccles. 5:3).

As with all the other ways God speaks, we must learn to listen to our spirit, not just the voice that speaks to us. I have been involved in much prophetic dream interpretation, and have learned to listen to God when He speaks to me in dreams, which He does frequently. Every night when I go to bed, I pray before I fall asleep. I always tell God that my body needs sleep, but He never sleeps. I ask Him to speak to me at night through a dream, He often does. I keep a dream journal and write my dreams down and pray over them. I must give a warning here. When God gives us a dream which is symbolic and needs to be interpreted, do not rely on a Christian dream interpretation book to interpret the dream. A book might be a helpful tool, but the interpretation must come through the Spirit of God. The dream comes supernaturally by revelation, so must the interpretation. It must come from God by revelation. This is what Joseph said when the prisoners told him their dreams:

> *And they said to him, "We each have had a dream, and there is no interpreter of it." So Joseph said to them, "Do not interpretations belong to God? Tell them to me, please."*
>
> —GENESIS 40:8

Through Other People

Sometimes we can be praying about something specific, and then someone will come up to us, say some random thing, and we *know* that God has just spoken to us and given us our answer. Or other times, we will turn on the Christian radio, and a song or some words from the announcer will hit our heart, and again, we just know it is God's voice to us. We can listen to a sermon, and it seems as if the preacher is speaking only and directly to us. Often God will use our leaders to speak to us if we can only open our spiritual ears and hear God speaking through them. Not everything people say to us is God speaking through them, of course. But the danger is that we get so familiar with each other that we miss God, as often happens with married people.

Our Natural Senses

One such example happened to a friend of mine who was flying to another city to preach. On the airplane, he suddenly smelled a very strong fragrance of fresh oranges. He looked around, and he could not see anyone with an orange or orange juice anywhere near him. Because he had learned to listen to the voice of God, he realized this must be God speaking to him. He asked God, and the Lord told him that the pastor's son in the church he was going to was very sick, and the doctors couldn't find the problem. God showed my friend that the source of the illness was a serious vitamin C deficiency. That was confirmed when he told the pastor what God had revealed to him. God used this to bring healing to the young man.

The important thing to understand is that God can use our natural senses to speak to us. But it must open our heart, and we must then receive His message in our spirit. You might walk into a meeting feeling fine and suddenly get a strong pain in a body part for no reason. That is one way the Lord might be telling you that He wants to heal someone who is suffering with exactly that pain or ailment. If this happens, ask Him and then listen in your spirit.

Visitations of Jesus

I have heard many testimonies about Muslims to whom Jesus has appeared, which resulted in their salvation. A visitation of Jesus is when Jesus Himself appears to us. It could be in a dream, a trance, or literally. This just shows the desire of God to speak to us.

Visitations of Angels

The Bible records many instances of angelic visitations throughout the Old and New Testaments. Many times, these angels had the purpose of bringing a message from God to the people. Sometimes they had a job to do, but often they just delivered a message. I have found 280 references in the Bible about angels, 178 alone in the New Testament. Here are some of them:

Then an angel of the Lord appeared to him, standing on the right side of the altar of incense. And when Zacharias saw him, he was troubled, and fear fell upon him. But the angel said to him, "Do not be afraid, Zacharias, for your prayer is heard; and your wife Elizabeth will bear you a son, and you shall call his name John. And you will have joy and gladness, and many will rejoice at his birth. For he will be great in the sight of the Lord, and shall drink neither wine nor strong drink. He will also be filled with the Holy Spirit, even from his mother's womb. And he will turn many of the children of Israel to the Lord their God. He will also go before Him in the spirit and power of Elijah, 'to turn the hearts of the fathers to the children,' and the disobedient to the wisdom of the just, to make ready a people prepared for the Lord."

—LUKE 1:11–17

Now in the sixth month the angel Gabriel was sent by God to a city of Galilee named Nazareth, to a virgin betrothed to a man whose name was Joseph, of the house of David. The virgin's name was Mary. And

77

having come in, the angel said to her, "Rejoice, highly favored one, the Lord is with you; blessed are you among women!"

—LUKE 1:26–28

Now an angel of the Lord spoke to Philip, saying, "Arise and go toward the south along the road which goes down from Jerusalem to Gaza." This is desert.

—ACTS 8:26

About the ninth hour of the day he saw clearly in a vision an angel of God coming in and saying to him, "Cornelius!" And when he observed him, he was afraid, and said, "What is it, lord?" So he said to him, "Your prayers and your alms have come up for a memorial before God."

—ACTS 10:3–4

Angels are never to be worshipped, as God alone must be worshipped. We should not seek the appearance of angels; we should always only seek God who is our Father in heaven, and who, through our Lord Jesus Christ, has given us free access to Him. I have had several encounters with angels, but the important thing is not to make angels or angel appearances the center of our focus, only the Lord Himself.

The Audible Voice of God

In my understanding, if God chooses to speak to you through His audible voice, it is to prepare you for a major task with possible opposition ahead. I have only heard God speak audibly once. It was not a pleasant, but a frightening experience, and it was very necessary because the job God had for me to do was with much opposition and cost a very high price.

> *So when the LORD saw that he turned aside to look, God called to him from the midst of the bush and said, "Moses, Moses!" And he said, "Here I am."*
>
> —EXODUS 3:4

> *Now when Moses went into the tabernacle of meeting to speak with Him, he heard the voice of One speaking to him from above the mercy seat that was on the ark of the Testimony, from between the two cherubim; thus He spoke to him.*

And the LORD spoke to Moses, saying: Speak to Aaron, and say to him, When you arrange the lamps, the seven lamps shall give light in front of the lampstand."'

—NUMBERS 7:89—8:2

And suddenly a voice came from heaven, saying, "This is My beloved Son, in whom I am well pleased."

—MATTHEW 3:17

The next day, as they went on their journey and drew near the city, Peter went up on the housetop to pray, about the sixth hour. Then he became very hungry and wanted to eat; but while they made ready, he fell into a trance and saw heaven opened and an object like a great sheet bound at the four corners, descending to him and let down to the earth. In it were all kinds of four-footed animals of the earth, wild beasts, creeping things, and birds of the air. And a voice came to him, "Rise, Peter; kill and eat." But Peter said, "Not so, Lord! For I have never eaten anything common or unclean." And a voice spoke to him again the second time, "What God has cleansed you must not call common."

—ACTS 10:9–15

Then he fell to the ground, and heard a voice saying to him, "Saul, Saul, why are you persecuting Me?"

—ACTS 9:4

No matter how God chooses to speak to you, it is always important. We should not seek one way above the other, but always have an open heart to hear what God wants to say to us. Through these pages I have wanted to show you that our God is a speaking God.

Chapter 8

Hindrances to Hearing God

Remember, we said that God's voice is like the radio waves; we need to learn to tune in, rather than try to convince God that He should speak. But there are things that can hinder us from tuning in clearly, or from developing the ability to hear God. Here are some of the biggest hindrances I have found.

Believing the Lie That You Are Not Special Enough to Hear from God

Many people, for various reasons, feel insecure and don't believe that they are worthy enough for God to speak to them. Since everything that we receive from God is by faith, we cannot hear Him if our heart is full of unbelief. Every single believer is special to God. We are His beloved children, for whom Jesus sacrificed His own life. Can you imagine a father who only speaks to some of his children, whom he has especially chosen, while the rest have to find out what he is saying through those specially chosen children? What kind of a father would that be? No decent father would ever do that. How much less will our Father in heaven do such a thing? He loves to speak to all of His children and has no favorites.

> *But from those who seemed to be something—whatever they were, it makes no difference to me; God shows personal favoritism to no man—for those who seemed to be something added nothing to me.*
>
> —GALATIANS 2:6

Comparing Ourselves with Others

Often people compare themselves to an experienced prophet or to people who have been prophesying for many years. If they don't prophesy as well, then they feel inferior and discouraged. This is very unhealthy.

God made all of us unique and different. In our spiritual growth we are all at different stages of maturity; therefore, it is never wise to compare ourselves with others. If we do that, we will easily miss hearing God many times because we expect Him to speak to us in the same way He speaks to these others. But God does not do that; He speaks in different ways to different people. He is after a relationship with us and wants us to develop the ability to hear Him well. Even in a human relationship, communication is developed through time. The more we grow in God, the more we learn to hear and distinguish His voice. Many people believe they have to prophesy just the way I do, and they measure themselves by me. This is a very unhealthy attitude. God made all of us very unique and individual. He is a God of incredible creativity. God doesn't want us to be clones of each other.

Fear That We Cannot Hear Him

Fear is the opposite of faith. Having a heart full of fear that we might not hear God correctly makes it harder for us to hear Him because our spiritual ears are closed to hearing His voice. When we come to God, we must approach Him without any fear in our hearts. When Jesus died, the veil in the temple was torn to show us that the way to God is open for everyone. We can come boldly to His throne of grace.

Seeing then that we have a great High Priest who has passed through the heavens, Jesus the Son of God, let us hold fast our confession. For we do not have a High Priest who cannot sympathize with our weaknesses, but was in all points tempted as we are, yet without sin. Let us therefore come boldly to the throne of grace that we may obtain mercy and find grace to help in time of need.

—HEBREWS 4:14–16

As we learn to discern His voice better, we will make mistakes because we are human. This must not make us afraid. As long as we stay teachable and walk in humility, mistakes will help us grow and mature in God. Fear will keep us from approaching God in freedom; therefore, we will have trouble hearing Him.

Lack of Trust

Often God will speak some very simple things to us. We have to trust that this is all He has to say. Many people find it hard to trust God when He chooses to say some very simple and basic things. Trusting God means we give up control and let Him decide what He wants to say to us and when.

One time God gave a lady I know a prophecy for another woman she had never seen before. The prophecy was simply that God loved her very, very, very much. The lady's own mind and emotions resisted the prophecy because it was too simple, so she didn't give it. But when the Lord rebuked her through another prophet, she eventually gave the woman the prophecy, and it literally saved her life. This woman was going through the most horrible circumstances and had decided to kill herself that day. She went to that church and said, "God, I am not sure if You love me. If You don't specifically let me know that You love me very, very, very much, I will kill myself on the way home." This woman was in the most desperate situation, and the simple prophetic word given in obedience saved her life.

Not Taking Time to Be Still and Remove Distractions from Our Lives

As mentioned before, this is a very important issue in the process of learning to hear God. How can we expect to hear God without taking the time to work on the art of communication, which implies *dialogue,* not just monologue? I have met Christians who are like teenagers, who only come to their parents to get the things they want, but are not willing to listen to the advice or the heart of their parents. This grieves the heart of God. He does not want us to use Him for information or things we can get from Him; He earnestly desires to walk in relationship with us. In part, this means not just speaking to Him, but also listening to what He has to say.

Today there are many wonderful gadgets and technical advancements, like iPads, iPods, iPhones, and Facebook, that make our lives easier and more efficient. However, often these become distractions that will hinder us from hearing God. We must learn where the off button is and use it frequently to quiet our hearts before God. We must be still in the presence of God, put all distraction and busyness on hold, and seek God's face.

Chapter 9

Three Safeguards

These are three safeguards that I have found very helpful in my walk with the Lord; they are part of His guidance to me about developing the ability to hear His voice better.

A Strong Relationship with God's Word

The Bible is the infallible Word of God. Even if everything changes, God's Word will never change. It has stood the test of time for thousands of years. We must love it, treasure it, study it, and read it regularly. A strong relationship with the Bible will protect us from strange and false prophetic words. The Bible says that heaven and Earth will pass away, but the Word of God will never pass away.

Heaven and earth will pass away, but My words will by no means pass away.
                                    —MATTHEW 24:35

If we know what God says in His Word, we will not be easily misled.

A Strong Relationship with the Church

The Bible speaks much about the body of Christ. No member can survive isolated on his own; he can only thrive as he is connected to the body of Christ. If we live our lives spiritually isolated, we are prone to deception which the enemy will bring into our lives. We must learn to walk in covenant relationship with the people God puts in our lives. Being a committed member of a church with healthy accountability will protect us from hearing and prophesying "strange things." We must not be satisfied with just going to a building once a week and meeting with other Christians. We must be connected through small groups and strong relationships with other believers.

Many Christians who are not connected to a local church have told me that they have their relationship with Jesus who is the head of the church; therefore, they don't need to be connected to people. But Scripture clearly teaches that we are all different members of the body and can only be connected to Jesus the head through each other. We need one another; it will help us to grow and keep us safe. How can the hand be connected to the head, unless it is first connected to the arm?

> *For as the body is one and has many members, but all the members of that one body, being many, are one body, so also is Christ. For by one Spirit we were all baptized into one body—whether Jews or Greeks, whether slaves or free—and have all been made to drink into one Spirit. For in fact the body is not one member but many. If the foot should say, "Because I am not a hand, I am not of the body," is it therefore not of the body? And if the ear should say, "Because I am not an eye, I am not of the body," is it therefore not of the body? If the whole body were an eye, where would be the hearing? If the whole were hearing, where would be the smelling? But*

now God has set the members, each one of them, in the body just as He pleased.
                                    —1 Corinthians 12:12–18

A Teachable Spirit

An unteachable spirit is what the Bible calls pride. God resists the proud but gives grace to the humble.

Likewise you younger people, submit yourselves to your elders. Yes, all of you be submissive to one another, and be clothed with humility, for "God resists the proud, but gives grace to the humble."
                                    —1 Peter 5:5

We must always be willing to be corrected. We must understand that no matter how closely we walk with God, and no matter what incredible revelations we may have received, we are still only fallible human beings. We must not just be willing to be corrected by God but also by people that God puts into our lives. This is a very important safeguard against errors in the prophetic. I will talk later about the importance of testing prophecy and how it should be tested.

As we develop our relationship with God and learn to hear Him better, we will find out that He is a speaking God. He loves to be involved in every aspect of our lives, and He loves to speak to us. Let me give a word of warning here: what God speaks to you personally is not for doctrine, but for application in your own life. It is not something you need to share with every member of the body of Christ. Doctrine must come from the Bible, not from personal experiences of hearing God.

Chapter 10

Who Can Prophesy?

The Difference Between the Gift of Prophecy and Being a Prophet

Before we answer the question biblically about who can prophesy, we need to understand the difference between a prophet and the gift of prophecy. What are the prophetic gifts, and what is a prophet? In First Corinthians 12:8–10, the Bible mentions nine spiritual gifts, three of which are considered to be the prophetic gifts. These are 1) The word of wisdom; 2) The word of knowledge; 3) Prophecy.

Since the purpose of this book is not a discussion of spiritual gifts, but of the gift of prophecy, I will concentrate only on this gift. The Greek word *prophēteúō* ("to prophesy") means to speak forth by divine inspiration. This could be with regard to the past, the present, or the future. Prophecy is not spiritual fortune-telling or card reading. It simply means to speak what God is speaking now. Prophecy is a gift that is available for individual believers. The Holy Spirit gives this gift at certain times for specific purposes, which I will talk about later. It is available for every Christian, which we will clearly see. Now that we have defined the gift of prophecy, let us define the role of the prophet.

We must not make the mistake of basing our beliefs about how prophets should be and what they should do on the Old Testament. If we make this mistake, we will be easily misled. Just as the Old Testament priests were very different from the priests in the New Testament, where every believer is now a priest unto God, so the prophet in the New Testament is also different. What is a New Testament prophet? There is not much mention in the New Testament about the prophet, so we have to take the few scriptures that God gave us. In Ephesians 4:11–16, the Bible teaches that God gave different ministries to the church, one of which is the prophet:

> *And He Himself gave some to be apostles, some prophets, some evangelists, and some pastors and teachers, for the equipping of the saints for the work of ministry, for the*

edifying of the body of Christ, till we all come to the unity of the faith and of the knowledge of the Son of God, to a perfect man, to the measure of the stature of the fullness of Christ; that we should no longer be children, tossed to and fro and carried about with every wind of doctrine, by the trickery of men, in the cunning craftiness of deceitful plotting, but, speaking the truth in love, may grow up in all things into Him who is the head—Christ—from whom the whole body, joined and knit together by what every joint supplies, according to the effective working by which every part does its share, causes growth of the body for the edifying of itself in love.

—EPHESIANS 4:11–16

The purposes of these ministries, including the prophet, are clearly described in this passage. They are for the equipping of the saints for the work of ministry, for the edifying of the body of Christ. (Eph. 4:12) The main purpose of the New Testament prophet is not to prophesy, but to equip Christians for the work of ministry.

Even though the main purpose of prophets is to equip the saints for the work of ministry, they also have a purpose beyond that. Because of the nature of the gift, they will be used to build up the church and challenge lukewarmness—or in other words, to separate the grey into black and white. They will inspire faith and growth in the people of God. Their ministry is never to draw attention to themselves, only to God. Prophets are entrusted with special revelation from God; therefore, God will hold them to a high standard, and they will often be under the strong discipline of God. We as a church must understand that, as with all ministries, their gift has nothing to do with their character. But because they have often been entrusted with strong revelation from God, He will deal very strongly with their character because their lives, as well as their revelation, have to be messages for God.

Prophets and their revelations must not be used to establish doctrine. Only the Bible is given to us for that purpose. However, God will often use them to reveal His specific and strategic will for a particular church or network of churches. Some Christians act like prophets know everything, just because many times God has given them astonishing insight and revelation. We must not make this mistake. They only know what God reveals to them. Often God will even hide information from them in order to keep them humble and to let the church understand that they only know what God shows them. This way they will remain dependent on God and each other in a healthy way.

No matter how much you pray for and desire to be a prophet, it will not make you one. Jesus gives these gifts to the church, as He sees fit. If God has chosen you to be a prophet, then the gift is not coming to you for you to use at specific times; you *are* the gift to the church. Whether you are asleep or awake, preaching or on vacation, you are always a prophet because this is what God has made you. In the same way, if God has called you to be a pastor, you will always be one, whether you are functioning as one or not at the moment. It all has to do with God's sovereign choice. You can either respond to this call of God on your life or reject it. You can work effectively in your God-ordained role, or ineffectively. People who are very sensitive, who have learned to hear God, and who have many revelations are often confused with prophets. However, we must not make that mistake.

The main purpose of the New Testament prophet is to edify the church and equip her so that every home can be a house of God and every member move in the prophetic. We must not make the terrible mistake of confusing the New Testament prophet with the Old Testament prophet. They have very different roles and functions. In the Old Testament, God mainly spoke to His people and leaders through the prophets. They walked in a very special relationship with God and heard Him very clearly. They often had to not just prophesy, but live their lives as a prophetic expression of what God wanted to communicate to His people. Hosea had to be married to a prostitute, for instance. Often God required very strange things of them in order to communicate a message to the people of Israel.

The main purpose of the Old Testament prophet was to bring God's message to His people, which was often a warning. In the New Testament we are clearly taught that every child of God can hear His voice. The main purpose of the New Testament prophet is to build up, train, and teach the church to hear and feel the heart of God, and to prophesy. Because of the nature of the gift that works within the prophet, he or she will naturally be used to give direction and vision to the church, as well as to bring strong prophecies. Often we have made the mistake of falsely labeling someone who prophesies a lot as a prophet. Prophesying does not make someone a prophet; that simply means that they have learned to be used in this precious gift, as we will see later. It is vital for us to understand that the New Testament prophet will often be used to speak strong words to the church, which might even include direction for the future. This does not, however, give the prophet authority to lead the church. This authority is given to the God-ordained leaders in that particular church. It is up to them to decide what to do with the message the prophet has released.

To be a true New Testament prophet, you must be called by God to be one, and you should be building up the church and equipping the saints. Over the last 30 years God has used me many times to speak His word about future things that He would do into the lives of leaders, churches, individuals with a specific calling on their lives, and even nations. This was not the gift of prophecy, which is available to every believer; God had used me as His prophet to bring specific words to these people in order to bring them into their destinies and release churches and leaders into their God-given purpose. However, I have also been used by God to equip, train, and release many, many people in different nations to flow in this wonderful gift of prophecy.

Chapter 11

Old and New Testament Prophets

A very common mistake, which I encounter regularly, is that when people talk about the ministry of the prophet they take their understanding of this ministry from the Old Testament. This is so common yet it keeps surprising me. I have discovered that the large majority of the Christians live their Christian lives with a mixture of the old and new covenant in their theology. This has been going on in the church at large for over 1700 years. The new covenant is so radical, that most Christians find it hard to embrace. I am convinced it is one of the strategies of the devil to infiltrate the minds of the believers with this evil that we are still living under the old covenant, because it affects every single area of our lives. And typically it changes the picture of who God really is, which robs us of our blessings, which Christ paid for on the cross.

The Role of the Old Testament Prophet

We must absolutely not model the ministry of the prophet according to Old Testament prophets. This is not only wrong, but also highly dangerous for every believer and can, and most likely will, lead to much pain and tragedies. This has been one of my great heartaches over the years, and something I have confronted often. When the church age, which is the age of grace, began God did away with the law and the prophets in their existing form and purpose. In the Old Testament, when the people of God or the kings, who were the leaders of the people then, wanted to hear from God, they had to ask the prophet who brought them "*the word of the Lord*". This was one of the roles of the Old Testament Prophet. But in the New Testament, we do not need a mediator for God to communicate to his children. Jesus said in John 10:2-3 that His sheep hear His voice

But he who enters by the door is the shepherd of the sheep. To him the doorkeeper opens, and the sheep hear his voice; and he calls his own sheep by name and leads them out

If you are a Christian, a sheep of our Lord Jesus, you can and should hear His voice for yourself and not run after prophets to hear His voice for you. Paul also says in Romans 8:14

For as many as are led by the Spirit of God, these are sons of God.

His Spirit, and the voice of our Lord Jesus, and not the prophets, must lead us as children of God. We open ourselves up to terrible deception if we see the New Testament prophet the same as the prophet was in the Old Testament. Demonic spirits can use anybody who opens themselves up to them and mislead the children of God who still believe in Old Testament prophets. History proves this in tragic ways. Just a few examples are: Joseph Smith, the founder of the Mormon Church; Mohammed, founder of the Islamic Church; Jim Jones, who many people followed into suicide, etc. Many people followed them because they claimed to be prophets and people who did not understand the Bible believed them to their own peril.

Another role of the Old Testament prophet was to confront and uncover the sin of the people of God. I was shocked when I arrived in Brazil in

2014 and a pastor told me that he was glad that I now live in Brazil. He told me that for sure God would now use me to confront and uncover the sin of the people in the church. I could hardly believe my ears and told him that I have never done that nor will I ever do it. That is not the role of a prophet in the New Testament. God has used me to bring powerful prophetic words in different parts of the world, but they were never to uncover or confront sin in the lives of His children. In the New Covenant God remembers our sin no more, because the blood of Jesus did away with it. In Hebrews 8:12-13 it says

> *For I will be merciful to their unrighteousness, and their sins and their lawless deeds I will remember no more." In that He says, "A new covenant," He has made the first obsolete. Now what is becoming obsolete and growing old is ready to vanish away*

If God doesn't remember our sins anymore, why should the prophet be used by God to uncover and bring it to the light? That would make God schizophrenic. He says, "I do not remember them anymore, but what I don't remember I somehow tell my prophets so that they can tell the people the things I said I do not remember anymore." Yet there are enough Christians who base their idea of a prophet on the model of the Old Testament prophet. They are impressed with the revelation some so-called prophets have, which often are very accurate, and therefore believe they are true prophets.

Understanding Prophetic Revelation

Revelation is not what makes you a New Testament prophet. Often these prophets are true prophets of God, but because they live with an old covenant mentality and mindset, they misapply their revelation and people get impressed with them. When God shows me negative future events that will take place, I usually never share them with anyone, just with my dear wife, who will not pass on that information. Only if God specifically tells me to release these revelations have I done so. You may wonder why then would God give his New Testament prophets such revelations? God gives this revelation to His prophets today for two reasons. Firstly, if God wants us to share, it is in order to prepare the people of God like the prophet Agabus did. In Acts 11:28- 29 we read

Then one of them, named Agabus, stood up and showed by the Spirit that there was going to be a great famine throughout all the world, which also happened in the days of Claudius Caesar. Then the disciples, each according to his ability, determined to send relief to the brethren dwelling in Judea

Here the disciples were able to be prepared and do something in order to help their Christian brothers. This was not declared as God's judgment, but simply as a fact about something that would happen.

Secondly, if God gives His prophets some revelation and does not want it to be shared, it is so that the prophets themselves can feel the heart of God and carry God's burden before His very throne and become an intercessor and an preventer of evil in this world. I personally believe that there is no true New Testament prophet who will not spend a major part of his life and ministry on his knees in the presence of God. Of course, the prophet looks much more impressive if he foretells major world or national events, does nothing about it in prayer, so it will truly come to pass. God taught me at the very beginning of my ministry about preventive prayer, which will never have a testimony here on earth, but only in heaven; because nobody will ever know what would have happened.

God has called me to Brazil to help Videira. It is not just to travel, preach, prophesy and pray for the sick, as some believe. It is also to spend many hours during many nights interceding for God's purpose to be fulfilled through Videira.

Chapter 12

Who Shall Prophesy?

This question has caused much argument in the church. It is my understanding from Scripture that *every Christian* can and should prophesy. Just as every Christian should be equipped by the other Ephesians 4 gifts (apostle, evangelist, pastor, teacher), so should every believer be trained by the prophets. Every church member should be a minister. Paul said to the Christians in Corinth that all *can* prophesy:

> *For you can all prophesy one by one, that all may learn and all may be encouraged.*
> —1 CORINTHIANS 14:31

All means everybody. The original meaning of the word *can* is to be able to. Every Christian has the ability to prophesy, but very few do so. I believe that this is because of a lack of teaching and understanding of this gift, and because of the lack of prophets doing their jobs in the church.

Just as it is the job of every one of the five ministry gifts to equip the Christians to do the work, the prophet is no exception.

Not every member is an evangelist, but every single member of the body of Christ is able to evangelize and reach people for Jesus Christ. This should be normal church life. Many evangelists have not understood this important task and have only focused on evangelizing the lost themselves, instead of raising up every single member of the church to do the work of an evangelist and reach the lost. I understand that for some people it will be more natural to evangelize, while for others, it will be more natural to teach those who have been led to the Lord. However, every single Christian without excuse needs to learn to be able to reach the lost. Every single Christian needs to learn to teach new believers the Word of God and how to live their lives before God. Does this mean that every believer has the ministry gift of a teacher? Of course not.

In the same way, you don't have to be a prophet to prophesy. This is not the point. However, just as every member should be trained in winning the lost, teaching them, understanding the apostolic purpose of the church, and pastoring new believers, so every member should be expected to learn to be used in the gift of prophesying. As it is with all gifts, some will be more naturally drawn to certain areas of ministry, but nobody is excused from winning the lost, and nobody should be excused from prophesying either.

I believe the meaning of this scripture is that God has given every believer the ability to prophesy at different times, whenever the Holy Spirit releases this gift to them. The Holy Spirit will release this gift in response to our earnest desire to prophesy. God says that we should *earnestly desire* to prophesy.

> *Therefore, brethren,* **_desire earnestly to prophesy_**, *and do not forbid to speak with tongues.*
> —1 CORINTHIANS 14:39, EMPHASIS ADDED

> *Pursue love, and desire spiritual gifts, but especially that you may prophesy.*
> —1 CORINTHIANS 14:1

God would never tell us to desire something that He does not want to give us. If God is saying that everyone *can* prophesy, and He wants us to *earnestly desire* to do so, then prophesying is for everybody, not only for some special people. God did not say this to a very specific group of people, but to everyone in the church; therefore, everyone who follows the instructions of the Bible will be frequently used to prophesy. I have seen this in all the churches I planted and pastored, as well as many other churches that I have ministered at. Our people regularly prophesied; there was a constant flow of this gift in all of our meetings and small groups. It was the normal thing to do because this is how I trained the people.

We have to understand that if the Bible teaches something and we do not see the experience of it in our own lives, we must not place the blame on God, or base our theology on our experience; rather, we must change our lives so that they match the teaching and truth of the Bible. Paul continues by saying that he wishes that all the members prophesied:

> **_I wish_** *you all spoke with tongues,* **_but_** **_even more that you prophesied_**; *for*

he who prophesies is greater than he who speaks with tongues, unless indeed he interprets, that the church may receive edification.

—1 CORINTHIANS 14:5, EMPHASIS
ADDED

Why would Paul say that he wishes that all Christians would prophesy if it were not possible for all do to so?

God puts the responsibility for being used in this gift of prophecy on us, although we cannot decide when and what we prophesy: that is God's choice. But He clearly puts the responsibility to be used in this gift on His children. Only by earnestly desiring it, as He said in His word that we should—only by burning with zeal and passion and crying out in prayer and even fasting to God to be used in this gift—will we be able to move in it on a regular basis. God gave the responsibility to cry out for it and earnestly desire it to us. Just as it is in the church, where most Christians sit in their chairs and let all the work be done by the pastors, instead of the pastors equipping and releasing the church to do the work, so it is with the prophetic ministry.

Too many Christians wait for heaven to move upon them in order to prophesy, but heaven is waiting for us to move upon it, so we can prophesy. Heaven is waiting and longing for Christians to take the Bible seriously and begin to earnestly desire to be used in this gift and get hold of all the resources of heaven, motivated by love for the church and the desire to edify the body. Then God will generously release this gift of prophecy to His children, and they will all prophesy just as Paul said we could.

In other words, God doesn't sovereignly activate the gift of prophecy in some children He has chosen to be fit and worthy. We activate heaven by our earnest, sincere, and burning desire to build up the body of Christ. I also must say that, sadly, I have seen many people desperate to prophesy because they want to be in the limelight; they desire to be important and feel special. This actually is in direct opposition to the biblical use of prophecy. When we pray in tongues, we edify each other; when we prophesy, we edify the church. This is why we should seek prophecy more than speaking in tongues—because we should love our brother and the church more than our own lives.

> *Let nothing be done through selfish ambition or conceit, but in lowliness of mind* **<u>let each esteem others better than himself.</u>**
>
> —PHILIPPIANS 2:3, EMPHASIS ADDED

If every member of the church would learn that, we would have a constant flow of the prophetic gifts. In fact, it would be impossible to see it released in a normal Sunday morning gathering because there wouldn't be time and space. Every time before I go and preach, I spend a lot of time crying out to God to use me in this precious gift of prophecy. I don't want people to be blessed by a man; this will not be of any lasting effect. I want God to touch them, speak to them, and change their lives. We all need to learn that nobody has the sacred right to stand before the people of God on behalf of God, before they have knelt before God on behalf of His people.

The Great Promise

God promises that He will pour out His Spirit upon *all flesh*:

And it shall come to pass afterward that I will pour out My Spirit on all flesh; **_your sons and your daughters shall prophesy,_** *your old men shall dream dreams, your young men shall see visions. And also on My menservants and on My maidservants I will pour out My Spirit in those days.*

—JOEL 2:28–29, EMPHASIS ADDED

Notice, this scripture says that "your sons and daughters will prophesy." It does not say some specially selected and chosen people will prophesy, but that sons and daughters will prophesy. Just as this promise of the gift of the Holy Spirit is for every believer, so prophesying is for every Christian too. In the Book of Acts, when the Holy Spirit fell upon *all the believers* that were gathered together, Peter quoted this scripture from Joel and said it was fulfilled that very day:

Then there appeared to them divided tongues, as of fire, and one sat upon each of them. And they were **_all filled with the Holy Spirit_** *and began to speak with*

117

other tongues, as the Spirit gave them
utterance.

—ACTS 2:3–4, EMPHASIS ADDED

For these are not drunk, as you suppose,
since it is only the third hour of the day.
But this is what was spoken by the prophet
Joel: "And it shall come to pass in the last
days, says God, That I will pour out of My
Spirit on all flesh; your sons and your
daughters shall prophesy, your young men
shall see visions, your old men shall dream
dreams. And on My menservants and on
My maidservants I will pour out My Spirit
in those days; and they shall prophesy.
—ACTS 2:15–17

Since Peter indicated that the promise of
Joel (which included prophesying) had been
fulfilled on the day of Pentecost, when all the
believers were filled with the Holy Spirit, we must
believe that prophesying is for all believers. Many
Christians, however, do not believe in the baptism
of the Holy Spirit and the speaking of tongues
because they have received inaccurate biblical
teaching; therefore, they never experience this.
Likewise, many believers never experience the gift

of prophesying as part of their Christian life. The promise of the Holy Spirit is not just speaking in other tongues, but also prophesying.

Chapter 13

How Can One Be Used in the Gift of Prophecy?

The Bible teaches us to *desire* spiritual gifts, *especially* that we may prophesy (1Cor. 14:1). The original Greek word translated "desire" in this verse is a very strong word; it means to burn with zeal, to pursue, and to strive for. Usually when I visit a church to do a prophetic seminar and teach the people how to flow in the gift of prophecy, I ask this question, "How many of you regularly prophesy?" Usually very few hands go up. When I ask the next question, "Who earnestly desires and burns with zeal to prophesy on a regular basis?" The same few hands go up. This *clearly* shows what the Bible teaches in First Corinthians 14: the ability to prophesy doesn't rest with God's sovereign choice but is linked to our desire to prophesy. It is not as some Christians firmly believe, "If God wants me to prophesy, then He will give me the gift of prophecy." And then they wait around for God to sovereignly hit them with prophetic words. These people usually never prophesy.

The first and most important condition for Christians to be used in prophecy is the earnest, sincere, and burning desire for God to use them in this precious gift. This does not mean that we can turn the gift on every time we choose to. Rather, as we earnestly cry out to God to use us in this gift, He will utilize us on a regular basis as He sees fit. How do we prepare to go to our small groups? Are we seeking God in prayer, crying out to Him to use us in prophecy? Do we seek His face and express our earnest desire and zeal to edify the church through this precious gift? This is what I do before I go to any meetings. Many times before a meeting, I spend hours on my knees, praying and crying out to God that He will use me and release the gift of prophecy so that the church would be built up, edified, equipped, and brought into her God-given destiny.

The Purpose of Prophecy

First Corinthians 14:3 says that "He who prophesies speaks *edification* and *exhortation* and *comfort* to men." These are three very important aspects of prophecy. Paul says that he who prophesies edifies *the church*.

He who speaks in a tongue edifies himself,
but he who prophesies edifies the church.
                           —1 CORINTHIANS 14:4

This is very important to understand. Prophecy is not so that the one who prophesies looks great or impressive, or so that people focus on the one who prophesies. It is not so that we can tell other Christians what to do with their future, where to move, who to marry, or which job to take. These things every Christian must find out from the Lord for themselves. Prophecy is to build us up; by doing so, the whole church is being built up.

As we saw earlier, to prophesy means to speak forth what God is saying now. Many Christians believe that prophecy *only* deals with the future and is only for giving direction. However, this is not biblical. In fact, it is very dangerous and unhealthy if we follow people in order to get a prophecy so that we know what to do with our lives and our future. We have the Bible as our guidance and the Holy Spirit who leads us into all truth and directs our lives. Prophecy can confirm what God is saying to us, but we should not treat it as a superstition or spiritual fortune-telling. It is the responsibility of every believer to find out direction for their life from God through prayer.

As mentioned before, New Testament prophecy is to edify, exhort, and comfort (1 Cor. 14:3). What does this mean? Let us look at these three words individually. *Edification* means to build up and promote someone's Christian growth. This is something that every Christian should desire to do. If we walk in love, our desire should be to always edify and promote the growth of other Christians, including the people of our church and small groups.

The word *exhortation* means to bring encouragement and consolation. It is the Greek word *paraklēsin,* which is related to the noun *paráklētos.* Jesus used this word to describe the Holy Spirit:

> *And I will pray the Father, and He will give you another Helper, that He may abide with you forever.*
>
> —JOHN 14:16

But the Helper, the Holy Spirit, whom the Father will send in My name, He will teach you all things, and bring to your remembrance all things that I said to you.

—JOHN 14:26

But when the Helper comes, whom I shall send to you from the Father, the Spirit of truth who proceeds from the Father, He will testify of Me.

—JOHN 15:26

Nevertheless I tell you the truth. It is to your advantage that I go away; for if I do not go away, the Helper will not come to you; but if I depart, I will send Him to you.

—JOHN 16:7

In all these verses, the Greek noun *parákletos* is used to describe the Holy Spirit. It means someone who draws near and helps, comforts, and encourages. Through prophecy, the Holy Spirit draws near to people in order to help and encourage them. Exhortation can also mean that which causes refreshment and consolation.

The third word in First Corinthians14:3 is *comfort*, which means to calm, comfort, strengthen, and give hope to. Here we clearly see that the purpose of prophecy is not to give direction, tell the future, or let people know what to do. It simply means that we hear from God the encouragement a person needs and speak that forth. It might have something to do with the future, but it doesn't have to. I believe that this gift should be manifested in every church on a regular basis. If every believer would let God use them in this gift in all of our small groups, there would be a constant flow of encouragement and Christian growth. It might be that through prophecy God will encourage people in their ministry or calling, but prophecy should never be treated just as telling people what to do with their lives and which decisions to make.

Chapter 14

Two Things That Grieve the Lord

Although God wants us to desire His gifts, there are two things that deeply grieve His heart. We must learn to understand these two things and avoid them at all costs.

Loving the Gifts More Than the Giver

There is a great danger that we seek the gifts above the giver. It is the Holy Spirit who gives the gifts of the Spirit, and God desires us to have these gifts and be used in them. This is a clear teaching of the Bible; however, if we love the gifts more than the Holy Spirit or the Lord Jesus, it is a very grievous thing to the heart of God.

Recently I traveled throughout many nations to preach for 49 days straight. My wife was unable to come with me because she was in university. It was very hard to be without her for such a long time. I was so excited to get back home and see her again. When I came home, all I wanted to do was just hold her in my arms without saying anything. If she had asked me to open my suitcase as soon as I got through the door to see if I had brought her any gifts, I would have told her that I missed her and just wanted to be with her. If she had insisted that she immediately see any gifts I had for her, it would have hurt me deeply. Of course I love to bring her gifts, but I am glad she wants my presence more than any gifts I can bring her.

Last year, I ministered in a church for 11 days straight. I had been preaching daily and praying for people, at times as much as three times a day. Every single meeting, I had seen God move; touch hearts; heal people, often dramatically and instantly from very serious diseases; save sinners; and give many powerful prophetic words. On Monday night, once again the room was packed with hundreds of desperate people, wanting a touch from God, desiring their broken bodies to be restored, and hopefully getting a miracle. The needs were great, people were desperate, and they had experienced the power of Jesus night after night.

But that night was different. As far as I was concerned, I did everything the same; I preached with a passion, called people to repentance, and prayed for crowds who knelt at the altar in tears.

Yet something was different. When I prayed for the first lady who was sick, she did not receive her healing miracle. I prayed harder; I rebuked, commanded, and did whatever one can do. I asked hundreds of people to stand with me in prayer, which they did, yet nothing happened. I wanted to speak words of encouragement to that lady and carry on praying for the other desperate people. I reached out in my spirit for prophetic words for the people, yet I couldn't. The Spirit of the Lord strongly restrained me. I had to tell the people, "Sorry, no more prayers," and I walked out of the room, leaving hundreds of desperate people behind.

As I returned to my hotel that night, I told the pastor not to pick me up for lunch the next day. I wanted to spend the whole day fasting, praying, and seeking God. I was unable to sleep. I cried, wept, prayed, and poured my heart out to the Lord. I wrestled most of the night with God until I finally was met by my beloved Lord Jesus Christ. What I experienced that night deeply impacted me and changed the course of the following night's meeting. Jesus showed me how deeply grieved He was about two things, and He wanted me to let these precious people in Brazil know.

The first thing that deeply grieved Him was that people began to seek the miracles more than relationship with Him. He showed me how He as the bridegroom longs so deeply for the His church, the bride. He has many gifts for her and loves to give them to her, but more than wanting His gifts, she must be consumed with passion for *Him*. Even if He would never bless her, never do a miracle, she must pursue Him above all gifts, experiences, and spiritual encounters. He let me feel the pain of His heart. I had been traveling for a while by then without my wife of 26 years; I missed her dearly and longed to be with her. However, as I lay on my bed in the early hours that morning, I found myself weeping, sobbing these words: "Jesus, I love You more than Debi; I desire You more than her. I long for Your presence more than for hers. I long for You so much more than I long for Debi. 'As the deer pants for the water, so my soul longs for You, Lord.'" Then He made me realize that He had let me feel His heart for the church. This is how much He longs for us, His bride. We must *never* exalt *anything* above our beloved Jesus—no miracle, no need, and no desire for anything. It is spiritual adultery from which we must repent. Although the Scriptures clearly teach and encourage us to earnestly desire spiritual gifts, especially that we may prophesy, we must not exalt the gifts above Jesus.

Secondly, people began to put their hope in me; they were pursuing me and hoping that once again God would use me to do a miracle. Jesus showed me how this also deeply grieves His heart. Our only hope is *Jesus,* not men or women, no matter who they are. In the church we have elevated preachers; we exalt them, follow them, chase after them, and put our trust in them, when Jesus is *everything* we need. He is our healing, wisdom, strength, understanding, and everything else. We spread the news about how great people are—how anointed, and how wonderful. All this grieves Jesus. He is all in all, and our hope for every miracle must rest in Him alone. He showed me also that, although I did not seek the glory and honor from men, I did not do anything to rebuke them for doing so, which grieved Him.

After I spent the night and the following day in my hotel room, feeling my own wickedness, shame, and sinfulness, and how I had grieved the heart of my Jesus, I went to the service that night. Again hundreds of desperate people were there. I tried to open my iPad for my sermon notes, but it wouldn't open. I stood on stage and nothing worked. I felt lost and desperate. Suddenly I realized that I must let Jesus do what He wants. So for the next hour or so I opened my mouth, and out poured a call for true repentance: a call to desire Jesus more than anything we think we need, a call to repent from elevating that little Austrian preacher and hoping that when he prays we will have a miracle and a touch from God. People crowded the altar, knelt, and laid down on the cold, stone floor with tears of repentance pouring down their faces.

After a while, maybe 20 minutes, I felt prompted by Jesus to tell them to go back to their seats. Then I called every single person who was sick and needed a touch from Jesus to the front. Dozens came to the front. I felt weak, hopeless, and lost. I was nothing; Jesus was everything. I felt Jesus tell me not to lay hands on anyone and not to pray for any individual person. So I prayed one single, simple prayer, and every single person, about 50 people, testified of being healed by some quite astonishing miracles, including a creative miracle. Bones shifted that night; immovable body parts moved again; chronic pain disappeared... The same things happened the next night in a different city. Jesus healed every person; eyesight was even restored.

Loving the Channel More Than the Source

In our immaturity, we can easily make the mistake to exalt the channel God uses more than God Himself. We must understand, no matter how powerfully God uses others, they are only the channel, and God is the source. All the gifts come from Him and not from us. The anointing is from God, not from us. Paul explained it to the immature Corinthians this way:

> *Therefore let no one boast in men. For all things are yours: whether Paul or Apollos or Cephas, or the world or life or death, or things present or things to come—all are yours. And you are Christ's, and Christ is God's.*
>
> —1 CORINTHIANS 3:21–23

Sometimes when I am in meetings where people exalt the ministers above God, I feel very grieved in my spirit. God will share His glory with no one, and one day we all will be judged by Jesus Christ—those who exalt the channels God uses and those ministers who seek exaltation from people. Think about the story when Jesus entered into Jerusalem on a donkey and all the people threw their clothes on the street, hailing their coming king:

> *They brought the donkey and the colt, laid their clothes on them, and set Him on them. And a very great multitude spread their clothes on the road; others cut down branches from the trees and spread them on the road. Then the multitudes who went before and those who followed cried out, saying: "Hosanna to the Son of David! 'Blessed is He who comes in the name of the LORD!' Hosanna in the highest!"*
> —MATTHEW 21:7–9

How stupid would it have been if the donkey had boasted to all the other donkeys when he got back to his stall that evening about how people celebrated him! They celebrated the Lord; he was only the one carrying Him. In the same way, we only carry the gift or the anointing. We are never the source; the Lord is.

Chapter 15

A Word of Warning

This does not mean that we can choose to prophesy to anyone that comes to us at anytime we would like to, as some people teach and believe. In fact, I believe that teaching is dangerous because it often causes people to prophesy out of their own soul or to draw from demonic inspiration. There is a very fine line between tapping into the Holy Spirit and into the demonic realm. Many people have received "prophecies" that were not true prophecies, and ended up frustrated, disillusioned, and disappointed. Because they believe that anyone can prophesy anytime they chose to, they now live with the pressure that they have to come up with a prophecy. When the Spirit of God doesn't speak, they draw things out from their soul, or even more dangerous, they open their spirit to deception. This should by no means discourage us from being used in prophecy; it simply makes us aware that there are times God is silent.

Scripture clearly teaches this in the context of the gifts of the Spirit and the gift of prophecy:

But the manifestation of the Spirit is given to each one for the profit of all: for to one is given the word of wisdom through the Spirit, to another the word of knowledge through the same Spirit, to another faith by the same Spirit, to another gifts of healings by the same Spirit, to another the working of miracles, to another prophecy, to another discerning of spirits, to another different kinds of tongues, to another the interpretation of tongues. But one and the same Spirit works all these things, ***distributing to each one individually as He wills***

—1 CORINTHIANS 12:7–11,
EMPHASIS ADDED

If we believe that we can choose when and to whom to prophesy, then in order not to violate Scripture, we have to look at the context and believe the same thing about the other eight gifts of the Spirit. Thus, we should also teach people that they can go and be used in the gifts of healing and miracles anytime they choose to. In this case, the hospitals should be empty because all we need to do is train people to release the gift of healing and miracles. We must remember that God wants *all* of His children to prophesy, and *all* can surely prophesy, but it is dictated by the Spirit and not by us.

Prophetic People

It is my personal belief that there are people who are prophetically gifted but are not prophets as mentioned in Ephesians 4. I call these the prophetic people. They are typically very sensitive, live in a very intimate relationship with the Lord, and have a highly developed prophetic gift. Some of them might be New Testament prophets who have not yet come into their calling and haven't developed fully. Others are simply people who have a stronger prophetic gifting than the average church member. These people are more keenly aware of the spiritual world and often feel the presence of demonic activity, as well as the presence of the Lord and angels.

The church at large has often made the mistake to leave the task of prophesying up to these people, simply because they have a more strongly developed gift. We do these particular people no favor if we elevate them and put them on a pedestal. It will cause them more harm than good. Many churches do not know how to handle these people, and they themselves often don't know how to use their gifts in a good and healthy way. Therefore, these highly sensitive people get used, abused, and wounded. They are treated as spiritual fortune-tellers.

Because these people are sensitive by nature, they fear rejection; they can easily give in to the temptation to give a "prophecy" to everybody who asks them for one. This can inevitably only end in disaster and pain for all parties involved because these "prophecies" can be easily drawn out of their own souls, or even worse, out of the demonic realm.

Sometimes these "prophecies" are not a result of hearing the Lord, but are born purely out of the pressure people have put on them. If these "prophecies" are wrong, then the anger and rejection from the people who pressured them to prophesy in the first place can be very fierce. This becomes a vicious cycle and makes many pastors shy away from the gift of prophecy and the prophetic ministry.

These prophetic people must also learn to distinguish when what God is showing them should be shared and when it should be a matter of prayer. God often gives these prophetic people special insight and revelation about certain things that are happening in someone's life, a church, or even nationally. Many times these revelations are not given so that they can be shared publicly, but so that the prophetic person can intercede for God's purpose to happen. Too many of these people have not understood the importance of prayer when these revelations come, and they go around telling other people about it, which causes much misunderstanding.

Prophetic people also must understand what God is saying to the church, other people, and to them. Because they have learned to hear God's voice and are sensitive to Him, they can often hear Him better than others. Therefore, many times God will say things to them which are meant *only* for them—for instance, something God wants to deal with in their personal lives and hearts. If they don't learn that not every revelation is to be shared, they will miss the point with what God is communicating. They need to learn to ask God if

He is speaking to them, someone else, or the church.

They also need to learn *when* revelation should be shared. Not everything God shows these prophetic people should be shared immediately; sometimes they need to wait to release the revelation at a God-given time. I remember when I was pastor in a church in Vienna; one day in the service; God gave me a prophetic word for a missionary couple that was part of our church. I wanted to share it with them, but the Lord prompted me not to say it. So I kept it to myself and just prayed about it. The word had to do with not being discouraged; the Lord wanted them to know that they were at the right place for now, and soon He would move them to another nation. The following Sunday when I came to the meeting, I received the same word for them, but again the Lord told me not to tell them. This happened for several weeks. Finally, many weeks later, I was released to give them the prophecy. After the meeting, they told me that everything was fine in their lives, but the weekend I prophesied to them, they had become discouraged, and it had to do with wanting to move to another nation. If I had given the prophecy many weeks before, it would have been the wrong time.

The Bible clearly says that we should earnestly desire to prophesy in order to build up our fellow Christians and the church, *but we should never chase prophetic words or people who prophesy.* Instead of earnestly desiring to prophesy, many Christians earnestly desire to receive a prophecy. This is the wrong way around. If we need to hear from God, no matter how desperate we are, we need to personally seek the Lord, trust Him to speak to us, and allow Him to do this in any manner He chooses. We have free access to His throne. As His sheep, we can hear His voice. It is unbiblical and can also lead to much pain and trouble if we treat prophecy as spiritual fortune-telling. Never chase people who prophesy or pressure anyone who God has used or uses in the gift of prophecy to give you a word from God.

I have experienced this pressure countless times in many countries and fight very hard to make sure that I don't give in to the pressure of people to prophesy, but only say what the Lord wants me to say. Every Christian needs to learn never to chase personal prophetic words for themselves. For those who do, trouble is on the horizon.

These highly sensitive and prophetic people often struggle with another problem which causes conflict in them and in their churches. Some do not understand that, while God may show us things concerning the future, it does not make us prophets. They may also have the tendency to take it personally when leaders and pastors who are responsible for leading the people of God don't feel the same way. Often God will show them things in order to pray, not to make decisions or pressure the pastor into making decisions. They need to learn to draw all their strength, support, and security from God. They must *never* use these revelations from God to manipulate anyone into doing what they feel is right. I will talk more about the importance of the right application of prophecy later.

I want to stress the point that I am absolutely convinced that we need these prophetic people. I believe every church needs these prophetic people who pursue the Lord and the prophetic gifts. Every pastor should pray for these people, encourage them, support them, and strengthen them. One reason why the church in many places in the world is not in good shape is because these wonderful, spiritually hungry people have not been supported and encouraged. Too often the baby has been thrown out with the bathwater. I encourage every prophetic person not to let negative experiences and wounds from the past stop them from pursuing the Lord and the prophetic gifts. Without these people, the church cannot reach her full potential.

Chapter 16

The Element of Faith

The Bible states that we should prophesy in proportion to our faith:

> *Having then gifts differing according to the grace that is given to us, let us use them: if prophecy let us prophesy in proportion to our faith;*
>
> —ROMANS 12:6

Faith activates the spiritual gifts just like everything else we receive from the Lord. Many Christians begin to sincerely desire to prophesy, but they expect God to put them in a state of ecstasy or trance where their mouth opens and out comes a prophecy. Just as when we are baptized with the Holy Spirit and God gives us the gift of speaking in tongues, we, in faith, speak out what the Spirit of God gives us. I have asked many Christians how they got filled with the Holy Spirit and began to speak in new tongues. I ask them if the Holy Spirit came upon them and used their tongue against their will, began to move it, and suddenly they just found themselves speaking in new tongues. They

144

all agreed that the Holy Spirit gave them the words, but they had to begin to speak out in faith what God gave them. In the same way, we must speak out in faith the prophecy that God bestows upon us.

Since we prophesy according to our faith, and faith grows as we use it, we can only grow in this gift of prophecy as we step out in faith and speak what God gives to us. Many Christians who begin in the gift of prophecy are afraid to step out and speak what God gives them because they compare themselves with someone who may have been used by God in this gift for decades, and they see themselves as falling short in this area. I understood this faith principle very early in my Christian life. I activated my faith over and over again. In many instances, God has given me a simple word or pointed out a person to whom He wants to speak. It is only as I open my mouth and step out in faith that God has given me astonishing prophecies for these people. Before I opened my mouth, I had only very few words for them. Sometimes I didn't even have a prophetic word, except the word that the Lord wanted to give them a prophecy through me. Often it took all the faith I had, in fear and trembling, to speak a word that only began to flow as I actually started speaking the first sentence to a particular person.

Faith is just like our muscles. It only grows as you begin to use it. The Bible says that every Christian has been given a measure of faith:

> *For I say, through the grace given to me, to everyone who is among you, not to think of himself more highly than he ought to think, but to think soberly, as God has dealt to each one a measure of faith.*
>
> —ROMANS 12:3

Some people seem to have so much more faith than others. This is because they constantly use their faith; therefore, it grows. This is the same with the gift of prophecy. Many people constantly step out in faith, using this gift; therefore, their faith constantly grows, and they prophesy more than others.

Every person reading this book was born with muscles. There is no exception. Why then do some people have much bigger muscles than others? It is because they use them more. They go to the gym and work hard. They take heavy weights and push against the pressure. This is not easy, and they often have pain. But they know that the only way to have their muscles grow is to push through the pressure of the weight and not give up. Faith is just like this, even faith in prophesying. The more you push through the difficulties, hardship, confusion, and doubt, the more your muscles of faith will grow, and the more God will be able to use you in this wonderful gift. I have been pushing a lot of spiritual weight over many years in this area; therefore, God was able to use me in many wonderful ways and change many lives, churches, and even denominations. Keep pushing through the doubt, and keep prophesying; it will make your muscles grow.

People who have been in meetings where I prophesied told me that I speak with such boldness, yet they have no idea of the fear and trembling inside of me, which I overcome by faith. We prophesy according to our faith. Don't ever copy someone else, or prophesy like someone else. You have to prophesy according to *your* faith. As you earnestly desire to prophesy, God will give you this gift and begin to use you. Faith only grows when it is used. As I taught this in churches and to people who have never prophesied, they overcame their fear and opened their mouths by faith, speaking out what God spoke to their spirit. I have seen incredible results; many lives have been changed and churches edified by people who have prophesied for the first time in their lives. Only practice makes us grow in the prophetic. Faith begins to take the first step before it sees the whole staircase.

Many people tell me that the main reason they don't prophesy is because they are not sure if the word is from God or themselves. They will never find out if they don't begin to speak and prophesy in faith. I will talk later about testing prophecy and being teachable and correctable. We learn by practice, not by knowledge alone. The whole Christian life is a life of experience and practice as we walk with God. It is the same in all aspects of the Christian walk.

> *For though by this time you ought to be teachers, you need someone to teach you again the first principles of the oracles of God; and you have come to need milk and not solid food. For everyone who partakes only of milk is unskilled in the word of righteousness, for he is a babe. But solid*

food belongs to those who are of full age, that is, those who by reason of use have their senses exercised to discern both good and evil.

—HEBREWS 5:12–14

The phrase "reason of use" here means to practice. So how do we grow spiritually mature? By putting things into practice. As we practice what the Bible teaches us, we grow spiritually mature. It is the same with the prophetic and the gift of prophesying.

We must not be afraid of failure; we must walk in faith, grow, and learn as we go along. We need to learn to give expression to our impression.

Chapter 17

Watch Your Motives

The motive for desiring to prophesy must never be anything else but love for the church. We have clearly seen that the purpose of prophecy is to build up the church; therefore, this must be our only motive. It is very interesting that the two main chapters in the Bible about spiritual gifts are First Corinthians 12 and First Corinthians 14. Right in between those two chapters, God put the great chapter of love—First Corinthians 13. In everything that God does in our lives, He is motivated by love. Therefore, our only motivation for desiring to prophesy must be love. We must never abuse the gift of prophecy to put ourselves in the limelight or to make ourselves look important. It is never about us; it is about Jesus and His church that He died for and so dearly loves. For that reason, we must constantly ask God to cleanse our hearts and search our motives. If we truly love the church of Jesus Christ and see what a wonderful effect the gift of prophecy has on her, we will earnestly desire to prophesy—not for ourselves, but for His bride, the church.

The Bible teaches much about love, also in the context of prophecy. It has deeply grieved my spirit how often I have seen people exalted who were used in accurate prophetic words. When God uses me to prophesy, it is never about me—only about edifying the church and helping people into their God-given destiny. We can easily test our motives by observing how we feel and react when God uses other people around us but doesn't use us, especially when He uses people we feel are inferior to us, which is only pride anyhow.

When God Is Silent

There are moments when God is silent and chooses not to speak. These are very hard times for prophetic people. It is a time of testing that the Lord will allow us to go through. Do we love Him more than the gifts? Do we still trust Him even when He refuses to answer our questions? All prophetic people must learn to deal with the moments when God is silent. In fact, we must learn not just how to handle these times, but how to love and treasure them. Moments of the testing of our hearts and the purifying of our motives are vital in our walk with God. We must not exalt the gifts above our character. Even the great prophet Elisha had to learn that.

In Second Kings 4, we read the story about Elisha and the Shunammite woman. This woman and her husband prepared a special guest room for the prophet to stay in whenever he was passing by. One day the prophet said, "What can I do for you? Shall I talk to the king on your behalf?" The prophet's servant told him, "She is without child." So Elisha prophesied that within a year she would have a son. The son was born and grew up, and one day he was in the field with his father, reaping the harvest. He suddenly got a strong headache and died.

The woman put him on his bed, and immediately said to her husband, "I want to go with one of the young man and the donkey to see the prophet." When she met the prophet on the mountain, something interesting happened. There was the prophet, with whom God communicated powerfully and regularly; even the secrets spoken in the king's chamber were revealed to him (2 Kings 6:8–12). Yet when the woman approached him, he made a very important statement:

> *Now when she came to the man of God at the hill, she caught him by the feet, but*

Gehazi came near to push her away. But the man of God said, "Let her alone; for her soul is in deep distress, **_and the LORD has hidden it from me, and has not told me._"**
—2 KINGS 4:27, EMPHASIS ADDED

Even the prophet had to accept that there are times when the Lord hides things from us and is silent in His love. These are very special and precious moments, but very hard for prophetic people who are used to hearing God on a daily basis. I have learned to especially treasure these moments as times where God deepens my trust in Him, brings me into His rest, and causes me to draw closer to Him in pure worship and adoration.

Chapter 18

How to Handle Prophecy

What Authority Does Prophecy Have?

It Is God Speaking Through People

As we have seen earlier, the word *prophecy* means to speak forth what God is saying; therefore, prophecy is the word of God. I have seen hundreds of lives changed, multitudes saved, and many miracles as a result of prophecies that people have received because the word of God carries authority. If it is a genuine prophecy, we have to treat it as a word that God Himself has spoken to us. Having said that, I believe we must understand that God speaks through imperfect human channels. This is why the Bible teaches us that we must test prophecy, which we will talk more about later on. But since it is God who speaks through prophecy, we must treat it as His word, not men's word.

Gifts Can Be Imparted Through Prophecy

The Bible teaches that gifts can be imparted through prophecy:

> *Do not neglect the gift that is in you, which was given to you by prophecy with the laying on of the hands of the eldership.*
>
> —1 TIMOTHY 4:14

Through prophecy God imparted a spiritual gift to Timothy. What does this mean? I have seen this happen many times. I have seen gifts of healing and other ministries imparted through prophecy. People who never had any plans to be used by God in certain gifts receive a word of prophecy and are promised that God will use them in particular areas with certain gifts. It could be working with children, being used in healing, or many other areas. Through this prophetic word, God has now imparted this gift and wants them to begin to grow in these gifts. Many people make the mistake of thinking that they now must wait for God to use them, rather than doing what the Bible says—not neglecting this gift, but beginning to use it and work with it. It is one thing for God to impart a certain gift through a prophetic word, but quite another thing to begin using this gift.

God Uses Imperfect Channels

Although prophecy is God speaking, we have to always understand that He uses fallible human beings, as mentioned earlier. Since none of us are perfect, we must understand that prophecies have to be tested. If prophecy was always 100 percent perfect, there would be no need for it to be tested as the Bible instructs us to do.

> *For we know in part and we prophesy in part.*
> —1 CORINTHIANS 13:9

Here Scripture tells us that even the most experienced people are not perfect and their prophecies have to be tested because they only know in part. In my experience, I have found that the church is much more gracious with people who practice other gifts than those who participate in the gift of prophecy. We don't expect pastors, teachers, or evangelists to be absolutely perfect and never make a mistake. While I do believe that people who prophesy should be accountable, we should also give them some grace and room to grow, understanding that nobody is infallible.

Prophecy Does Not Carry the Same Authority as the Bible

God has given us the Bible as the infallible Word of God. No prophecy should be given equal or greater authority than Scripture. Only the Bible is the infallible Word of God.

Prophecy Must Be Tested

Here are two very important scriptures regarding prophecy that we have to understand if we want to see our churches and small groups released and flowing in the gift of prophecy:

> *Do not quench the Spirit. Do not despise prophecies. Test all things; hold fast what is good.*
> —1 THESSALONIANS 5:19–21

Paul clearly instructs us here that we must not despise prophecies, and we must test all things. Why would he give us this instruction? Why does Paul put the testing of all things in the context of not despising prophecy?

157

I believe that because some prophecies were released from the flesh rather than from the Spirit of God, prophecy has been despised in many churches. This is never the appropriate approach. The answer to abuse is never *no* use, but the *right* and *correct* use. This is the same in all areas of our Christian lives. Pastors often overreact instead of taking the advice of the apostle Paul, who told us to test all things and hold on to the good, rather than despising prophecy because of bad experiences. Here is the second important scripture.

> *Let two or three prophets speak, and let the others judge.*
>
> —1 CORINTHIANS 14:29

The word *judge* here does not mean to judge in the sense of criticizing, but rather in the sense of examining something to see if it is real, to make sure that it is a true word from God. The very fact that God tells us to test prophecy means that there can be prophecies in the church that are not truly the word of God. Therefore, we should learn to test prophecies, while remaining open to the gift of prophecy even when we have encountered prophecies that did not pass the test.

The scriptural command is to not despise prophecies just because some have been wrong, but to hold onto the good. If we learn to follow the advice of the apostle Paul and only prophesy what edifies, comforts, and encourages, then the whole church will be built up.

Chapter 19

How to Test Prophecy

Test It by the Bible

Any prophecy that goes against the written Word of God must be rejected. God will never contradict His own written Word. God's Word will endure forever. When testing the prophecy by the Bible, we must not pick one verse out of context in order to prove the prophecy true. The prophecy must line up with the whole teaching of the Bible. If the Bible doesn't say anything about the specific topic within the prophecy, then we must make sure nothing in Scripture contradicts it. I have heard people prophesy that God understands the hardship they are going through in their marriage, has seen how long and patiently they have suffered, and has freed them to divorce their spouse. The Bible teaches that God hates divorce; therefore, this prophecy doesn't pass the test of the Bible and needs to be rejected. At any given time, when a prophecy contradicts the Bible, it has failed the test of being a true prophecy.

But what if the Bible doesn't say anything about the subject that was prophesied? People have told me that the prophecy has to be false because there is no teaching in the Bible that mentions what has been prophesied. The question is not whether the Bible talks about what was prophesied, but whether the prophecy contradicts Scripture in any way. I tell these people that the Bible doesn't say anything about cars, airplanes, and washing machines either; therefore, they should reject these items, wash their clothes by hand, and walk instead of driving or flying.

Prophecy Must Not Create Fear

We have seen earlier that prophecy is for edification, encouragement, and comfort. So prophecy must never make people afraid. Even if God were to warn us in a prophecy, there would be hope and faith attached to it, and it would not leave us in fear. The fear of God is a healthy fear that will draw us closer to Him and bring repentance and change in our lives. The devil operates in the realm of fear and controls people through fear. God is love and operates in the realm of love. I firmly believe that God disciplines His children, and all wise and mature children of God will constantly seek His discipline and ask for wisdom to respond rightly to His discipline. This has been my constant prayer since I was a teenager, and it will be my prayer until the day I die. However, it is not the purpose of prophecy to bring discipline to the church. The Father disciplines His children, and God has entrusted church leadership with the discipline in the local church, not the gift of prophecy.

Many times I have seen people abuse prophecy to correct people publicly or make them feel bad and afraid. I don't believe this is biblical prophecy, but comes from the flesh.

Do Not Judge Prophecy in the Flesh

Sometimes God will say something to us that goes against our natural ability or desire. We must not judge a prophecy by whether or not we can imagine it being fulfilled. God wants us to walk in *His* strength, not our own. Some things that God has spoken to me through prophecy seemed impossible to see fulfilled. When God told

Abraham he would have a son, it was humanly impossible. Throughout the Bible, we observe that God delights to use weak channels to fulfill His purposes. Over and over again, we see that where things are humanly impossible, God's possibilities begin. This is the life of faith that God has called us to. We must always remember that nothing is impossible with God; the test is not whether we feel that it is possible to see the prophecy fulfilled in our life.

Test It in Your Spirit

We test the prophecy in our spirit, not in our soul. God's Spirit dwells in us, and He will witness to our spirit if the word spoken is of God or not. If you have a bad and uneasy feeling in your spirit, just put the prophecy aside. If in your spirit you feel that it is wrong or you feel a lack of peace, just put the prophecy aside. Sometimes people test a prophetic word by the Bible, and there is nothing against it. They don't have a witness in their spirit, but they also don't feel anything against the prophecy and don't know whether to receive it as from God or not. In this case, just put it aside for the moment and ask God to confirm it. The Bible says that by two or three witnesses all truth will be established (2 Cor. 13:1).

It is not a sign of weakness or lack of faith if we ask God to confirm His word to us if we are unsure. God loves His children, and if we ask Him with a sincere heart to confirm if the prophecy is from Him or not, He will gladly do so. Many times when I have taught this, people have told me that they received the same prophecy from a different person who knew nothing about it.

Check with God-Appointed Leaders

If we are not sure whether a prophecy is from God after we have tested it by the Bible and in our spirit, we should talk to the leaders whom God has placed in our lives. Often God will give them supernatural wisdom, and they will see things we cannot see. The important thing is that we are humble and teachable.

God desires for us to walk in covenant relationship with one another and has placed structure and authority in the church for a reason.

Once a Prophecy Has Passed the Test

Once we have tested the prophecy and decided it truly is a word from God, we must not let the enemy rob it from us and change our mind in difficult times. Prophecy must not be tested by circumstances in difficult times, but by all these ways we have just mentioned. When God speaks, He always desires for us to see His word and promises fulfilled. But we must learn to work together with God and His purposes in order to see His will and promises fulfilled.

When I began to plant churches almost 30 years ago and ministered in the prophetic gift, I became very frustrated and wanted to give up on the prophetic ministry. I have seen so many people who received a prophecy and then lived their lives carelessly, not walking earnestly with God. Often, their attitude was that now they had received a great prophecy, it didn't matter how they lived their lives. This grieved my heart so much that I wanted to quit prophesying. But I have decided that I will teach the people of God how to do it right rather than give up.

Throughout the Bible we find this wonderful mystery of God and men and women working together. God will not do the things that He wants *us* to do. He has a purpose and wants us to work together with Him in fulfilling this purpose and seeing His Kingdom established. When we receive a prophecy, it is where the journey begins, not ends. This is when our part begins.

Chapter 20

The Road of Contradiction

Why the Opposite of the Prophecy Sometimes Occurs

After we receive a prophecy, it is possible that the opposite of what was promised can happen. I call this the road of contradiction. God will take us down this road many times, and every believer has to learn to walk this road. When we are on the road of contradiction, we must understand some important truths. What we must never do is test the prophecy by the changed circumstances when we are on this road of contradiction. We test it when we receive it in the ways I have described, *not* after a while when we are on the road of contradiction. Many people in the Bible had to walk the road of contradiction after they received promises from God. Once we have tested the prophecy and are sure it is from God, we must understand that God doesn't change His mind. Why does God sometimes take us on this road of contradiction? Why does He allow the opposite of our prophecies and promises to happen? Here are some reasons.

The Importance of Our Character

Throughout the Bible, we see that God gave people a dream or a promise, and then He started to work on their character. If we do not have the character to inherit our prophecy, we can cause great damage in the Kingdom of God. God gave Joseph the prophetic dream that his family would bow down to him, but the opposite happened; his family sold him into slavery, and Joseph ended up in prison. God gave David the promise that he would be king, and the prophet even anointed him, but instead of being in a place of authority, he had to run for his life, chased by a king who tried to kill him. God gave the people of Israel the promise of a land of milk and honey, but then they had to walk through the wilderness. These are just a few examples which we find throughout the Bible. When we are on the road of contradiction, we must ask God if He is trying to teach us anything and wants to work on our character. We must completely surrender to Him and allow Him to do whatever work needs to be done in our heart. Our heart must remain teachable and surrendered to His will and discipline. When Joseph first received the prophetic dream that his family would bow before him, he was a proud young teenager. But it was on the road of contradiction, where the opposite of his promise happened, that God formed his character. In the prison of his circumstances, God did a deep work in his life. When the prophecy was finally fulfilled, he had a godly character and walked in love, being used to fulfill the purpose of God in his life.

God's Foreknowledge

In First Timothy, Paul counsels Timothy that he should fight the warfare with the prophecies that he has received:

This charge I commit to you, son Timothy, __*according to the prophecies*__ *previously made concerning you,* __*that by them*__ *you may wage the good warfare.*
—1 TIMOTHY 1:18, EMPHASIS ADDED

Sometimes God gives us a prophecy because He knows the opposition that is coming in the future. When we face opposition, we can use the prophecy as the word of God and declare it, claim it, and fight with it until we see the promise fulfilled.

I know two men who were in ministry together. One day when they were speaking at a conference in Europe, God told one of the two men, who is a prophet, to go and buy an expensive bottle of wine for his friend, the other minister. So he went to town and did that. As he handed the bottle to his friend, God gave him a prophecy that the best years of his life were ahead of him, just as he was now receiving the best wine. A few months later, the man who received the wine was diagnosed with cancer, and the doctors said there was no

169

hope of survival. The opposite of the prophecy happened; he was on the road of contradiction.

When the prophet heard the news, he told his friend not to doubt the prophecy just because the circumstances had changed and it seemed to be untrue. He told him to take the bottle of wine, look at it, and fight the fight with the prophecy God had given him. Every day this man fought the warfare and declared, "I will not die, because God said that the best years of my life are still ahead of me." Now, many years later, this man is still alive. The prophecy was not false. God knew the future, and in His foreknowledge gave the man the hope and a word of prophecy that he needed in order to fight the battle. This man did the right thing; instead of testing the prophecy months later by his circumstances, he held on to it and saw the victory. When God gave him the prophecy, He already knew that in a few months there would be trouble in his life, so He gave him a prophecy to fight with.

The Opposition of the Devil

As Christians, we are in a spiritual battle. The devil does not want us to be successful and victorious. He will throw things against us that will oppose the prophecy we received. Every word of God has the power to completely transform our lives; since prophecy is God speaking to us, the devil hates prophecy. He will often try to bring opposing circumstances in our lives or sow doubt concerning the word of God. At such times we must not test the prophecy and doubt it (that should have been done when we received it). Now we need to take the prophecy and fight our warfare. We need to stand in the face of opposition and boldly declare what God has spoken. It is our faith that is the victory that overcomes the world. Our words have creative power, and often in times like these, Christians let go of their prophecy and abort their God-given promises.

In theology there is a term called the "law of first mention." It basically says that if we want to understand a theme in the Bible and interpret it correctly, we need to find out where it is first mentioned. The first mention of *speaking* in the Bible was not to communicate, but to create:

> *In the beginning God created the heavens and the earth. The earth was without form, and void; and darkness was on the face of the deep. And the Spirit of God was hovering over the face of the waters. Then*

God said, "Let there be light"; and there was light.

—GENESIS 1:1–3

Speech was originally used to create, not to communicate. While communication is important, we must also understand the creative power of our words. In times of opposition, we must boldly confess the prophecy God gave us, and on the road of contradiction, we must declare it and see it come to pass.

Chapter 21

The Three Elements of Prophecy

Revelation

The first part of prophecy is revelation. Prophecy comes to you by divine revelation; it has nothing to do with your knowledge or information. We need to be very careful that we don't mix prophecy with our own wishes or desires. It needs to be pure revelation from the Spirit of God. If our motives are not pure, or if we want certain people to do specific things, we can mix a true prophecy with our own desires, making the prophecy impure. We must make sure that what we speak is coming to us by revelation, not from our own soul.

Interpretation

The second part is interpretation. Interpretation entails an understanding of what the prophecy means. Sometimes God speaks clearly and directly; other times He speaks in symbols, pictures, or words that need to be interpreted. God told Abram directly that he would have a son, but He told Joseph through dreams that he would save his family and his people. This is where people often make mistakes. Just as the prophecy must come by revelation, the interpretation must also come by revelation. When it comes to interpreting prophecy, there is the danger of beginning in the Spirit and then continuing in the flesh. The Galatians were in danger of doing this in their Christian walk.

> *Are you so foolish? Having begun in the Spirit, are you now being made perfect by the flesh?*

Since the revelation is from God, the interpretation must also come from God. If we do not have the interpretation given by the Holy Spirit, we must only give the prophecy (revelation) to the people we are prophesying to, and leave the interpretation up to them. Often they already know it. Other times, God specifically speaks to them in a way that prompts them to seek God for the interpretation because He wants to draw them close and desires for them to seek Him.

One time God gave me a prophetic vision for a young lady. I saw her praying and crying out to God, and then pointing to a young man and crying out to God again. Then God gave me the following prophecy: "God has heard your prayers and will answer it, but it is not the right time yet. You have to wait three more years." I thought to myself that the interpretation was that she was praying and asking God to give her this young man as a husband. But I understood that these were merely my own thoughts and not the interpretation that came to me by revelation from God, so I only gave her the vision and prophecy. I had learned not to say anything if God does not give me the interpretation by revelation.

After the service, this young woman came to me and introduced her husband to me. They had just been married recently, and she wanted a baby quickly, but her husband said he believed they should wait for three years. She had been praying for God to change the mind of her husband. When she received the prophecy, she knew exactly what it meant, and now she was at peace because she knew it was the will of God for her to wait. I was surely glad I did not speak out what I thought the interpretation was

Application

We have to understand that application is an important element of every prophecy. Only when we learn to work together with God will His word and His plans for us be fulfilled. It is always exciting to receive a prophecy or a promise from God, but that is when the hard work begins. We must learn to work together with God. Faith without works is dead. God never gives us a prophecy just so we feel good or are excited, but so we will work together with Him to fulfill His purposes for our lives and glorify Him alone. Paul said we must work out our salvation, but God works in us. Throughout history and the entire

Bible, we see the working together of God and men and women in order to have the plans of God fulfilled.

> *Therefore, my beloved, as you have always obeyed, not as in my presence only, but now much more in my absence, work out your own salvation with fear and trembling; for it is God who works in you both to will and to do for His good pleasure.*
> ——PHILIPPIANS 2:12–13

The application must always be left up to the person who received the prophecy, never to the one who gives the prophecy. If we do not understand this, we can easily try to manipulate people using prophecy, which is a terrible thing to do. The person giving the prophecy is just like the mail man who brings the mail. His job is to deliver the mail to me, not to make sure that I open my mail, pay all the bills, and answer every letter. If the mail man tried to put pressure on me to do all these things, I would tell him to leave my house and not to interfere with my life. Once he has delivered the mail, his job is done.

This is how we must treat prophecy. Even the prophet Agabus in the Bible did it this way:

> *And as we stayed many days, a certain prophet named Agabus came down from Judea. When he had come to us, he took Paul's belt, bound his own hands and feet, and said, "Thus says the Holy Spirit, 'So shall the Jews at Jerusalem bind the man who owns this belt, and deliver him into the hands of the Gentiles.'" Now when we heard these things, both we and those from that place pleaded with him not to go up to Jerusalem. Then Paul answered, "What do you mean by weeping and breaking my heart? For I am ready not only to be bound, but also to die at Jerusalem for the name of the Lord Jesus." So when he would not be persuaded, we ceased, saying, "The will of the Lord be done."*

—ACTS 21:10–14

Here we see no indication that the prophet Agabus used prophecy to manipulate Paul into what he thought he should do. All he did was deliver the prophecy. Even when the other brothers tried to convince Paul to apply the prophecy in a certain way and not go to Jerusalem,

Paul refused to do so. It was up to him to apply it correctly. I have seen people fall into this error many times. They receive a prophetic word for someone, but because they don't understand this important part of application, they try to tell people what to do and how to act according to their prophecy. This is not their job to do. The application is left to the one who received the prophecy.

Chapter 22

Important Truths to Understand About Prophecy

God Fulfills His Word

Although we need to work together with God, we must remember that it is *God* who fulfills His promise. It was God who gave Abraham his son, promoted Joseph to the throne, gave David the kingdom, and brought His people into the Promised Land. Our part is to work *with* God, but we have to trust God that He will do what He has promised. By faith we inherit God's promises. If we don't understand this, we will end up like Abraham and produce an Ishmael. We have to learn to apply our prophecies and work with God, but keep the balance of faith and works. It is our faith in the word of God that will release His power and bring to pass whatever He has promised us.

God's Promise Is His Plan, but Not His Guarantee

God promised the whole nation of Israel a great land where milk and honey was flowing, but most of them never received the promise. God's promises have conditions; they require our obedience, our faithfulness, and our submission to the will of God. Most of the people of Israel never received the promise because of their evil hearts of rebellion and unbelief.

I have seen countless prophecies aborted because people had a careless attitude toward the prophecy they received. Paul told Timothy to fight with the prophecy; we must do likewise. We must stand in faith, surrender our hearts to God, withstand the enemy, and work together with God in full obedience in order to see the prophecy fulfilled.

Understand God's Timing

God's timing is different than ours. He lives in the realm of eternity and sees the end from the beginning.

> *For a thousand years in Your sight are like yesterday when it is past, and like a watch in the night.*
>
> —PSALM 90:4

The Bible says that we need *faith and patience* in order to see our promises fulfilled:

> *And we desire that each one of you show the same diligence to the full assurance of hope until the end, that you do not become sluggish, but imitate those who through faith and patience inherit the promises.*
>
> —HEBREWS 6:11–12

Many Christians have faith but no perseverance. Faith alone will not give us our inheritance and the fulfillment of our prophecies. God told Abraham that He would give him a son. Ten years later, he still did not have a son. Some prophecies that I havereceived from God were fulfilled quickly; others took more than ten years to be fulfilled. Never let the passing of time cause you to forsake the prophecy that God has given you. Often we need to pass the test of time before we can see the promise God has given us. During this test of time, God searches our hearts, purifies our motives, and teaches us many valuable lessons.

Beware of the Spirit of Control

We must never manipulate people by using prophecy. It is important that we don't bring into the prophecies our own agenda or desires. God never manipulates His children. He speaks His word but gives us the free will to obey or disobey Him. If we use prophecy to manipulate other people, we open ourselves up to the influence of evil demonic spirits and deception.

When I started to plant the first church, I was very young. We spent a lot of time in fasting and praying. There was a very sweet older lady in our church who loved me very much like a mother. She was always very concerned about me, and one day she told me that I must eat more and not fast so much. I thanked her for her advice, but told her that I needed to do what I felt the Lord wanted me to do. She was very frustrated that I didn't take her advice. Then she began to prophesy to me, telling me that the Lord had told her I must not fast so much. She was sweet and started out very sincere, but got into a dangerous area when she tried to manipulate me.

Don't Suddenly Change the Direction of Your Life

Just because you receive a prophecy doesn't mean you are to leave everything and change the direction of your life based on that one prophecy. If prophecy confirms what God has already spoken to you regarding a new direction, then follow the leading of the Lord. But if you receive one prophecy telling you to forsake everything and move or marry or make some major change, *do not do it*

Don't Prophesy Relationships and Marriages

God must tell people who to marry and spend the rest of their lives with. When I was pastoring churches, we always taught people never to use prophesy to try to get people into a relationship with each other. Marriage is a very holy thing and must be treated as such. God knows best how to bring people together, and He is well able to tell them. Because of my prophetic ministry, many times God has shown me who would get married in the church where I was the pastor—often God told me years ahead. I never said anything, or even gave a hint. I just prayed for God's will to be done. When people came to me, saying that God had told them they should get married, and asking what I thought about it, I never told them what I knew. I always told them that they needed to know from God.

The Importance of a Pure Channel

Prophecy is the Spirit of God speaking through us. God is perfect, but we are imperfect. The condition of our heart and motives is very important in prophecy. We must die to our own selfish desires every day. It must be our constant prayer for God to purify our heart and motives. It is my permanent prayer for God to purify the prophetic gift in me, to search and cleanse my heart, and to purify my motives. If our motives are not pure, we will mix the word of God with our own thoughts and wishes.

Don't Prophesy People's Desires

When it comes to prophesying, we must learn to hear only what God is saying. Often people will try to put pressure on those who prophesy to say what the listeners want to hear. We must never give in to this pressure. We must say only what God says, no more and no less, whether the people like it or not. Some very tender-hearted and sensitive people are especially prone to giving in to this temptation.

If we believe that everything that comes to our mind is a prophecy, we will be in great danger. If people have learned to be very sensitive to the spiritual world, they can easily feel the desires of other people and confuse it with prophecy. This can even look very impressive, but it is not the Spirit of God speaking to them. We must not try to come up with a prophecy, or put pressure on ourselves to always have a prophecy. If we earnestly desire to prophesy, God will use us in prophecy. He wants all of His children to prophesy. But it is the Holy Spirit who gives you the prophecy at the right time.

I have met many people who teach and believe that we can always choose to prophesy when we want; we just speak what comes to our minds. I believe this is a very dangerous and false teaching.

Chapter 23

Practical Applications

Dramatic or Edifying?

God never gives us a prophecy so that we look important. When we prophesy to people, we must always remember that it doesn't matter if we look important or not. Only two things matter: 1) God must be glorified; 2) People and the church must be blessed and edified. We must never make our prophecy more dramatic than what God is saying. It is never about us. It's all about God. We are nothing but a channel in the hands of Almighty God.

No Secret Prophecies

If God gives you a prophecy, don't go into a corner of the room and prophesy privately. This is where many problems arise. Often things are misunderstood or heard in a wrong way. Prophecy should be spoken publicly so that others can judge. If God does give you a prophecy that is very personal, take someone along with you to the person you are prophesying to. Always avoid prophecies in secret.

The Danger of Unhealed Wounds

We all get wounded as we walk through life. The question is how we deal with those hurts and wounds. If we don't allow the Lord to heal those wounds, we will filter what we hear from God through our own pain and experience. This can cause the prophecies that we give to be distorted. We must always trust God to heal our wounded hearts so that the prophecies can come forth as pure.

The Importance of Accountability

Spiritual authority is very important in the church of Jesus Christ. For everything we do, we must be accountable to someone. God has set authority in place for a reason; it is for our protection. No matter how experienced we are in the gift of prophecy, we must always remain accountable and open to correction. When we prophesy publicly, we should be willing to be corrected publicly. God always honors humility. How shall we learn if we are not tested? Keep practicing and learn to be corrected.

I pray that the pages of this book will help release the people of God to learn to prophesy in their small groups and any other settings so that the church can be edified and God will fulfill His purpose in the Earth.

REINHARD HIRTLER